AN ENGLISHMAN IN THE MIDI

John P. Harris lives with his beautiful clever wife in a crummy house in an obscure part of southern France. When they lived in England he taught French and English. Ten years ago he started writing. His published work includes articles in French and in English, and books in English. The Harrises have two children, two grandchildren, no cats and several mice.

AN ENGLISHMAN IN THE MIDI

John P. Harris

Drawings by Llewellyn Thomas

BBC BOOKS

Published by BBC Books,
a division of BBC Enterprises Limited,
Woodlands, 80 Wood Lane, London W12 0TT

First published 1991

ISBN 0 563 36229 4

Set in Itek Meridien by Ace Filmsetting Ltd
Printed and bound in Great Britain by Clays Ltd, St Ives plc
Cover printed by Clays Ltd, St Ives plc

CONTENTS

PREAMBLE

The chapters of this book are expanded versions of talks broadcast on Radio Four in the summers of 1990 and 1991. I would like to dedicate them to a modern Svengali, 'my' producer Merilyn Harris. Although she is a paragon of tactful kindness, apparent enthusiasm, firm discipline and good taste, we are not related.

I am grateful to the editors of *Le Monde*, *The Times* and *She*, in whose pages fragments of these chapters appeared, in different form. I am also grateful to Michael Alexander, co-author with the late Giles Romilly of *The Privileged Nightmare*, for permission to quote from that book.

Villages like the one described here certainly exist. So do their inhabitants. I shall never be able sufficiently to thank the citizens of a certain Languedocian village for the kindness, hospitality and tolerance that they have showered upon my wife and myself for many years. But I have shuffled the cards, and I had better affirm that any resemblance to living persons is coincidental. (Indeed, my wife sometimes maintains that I am a figment of her imagination.)

How to Wind a Clock
and Get Integrated

We've got a clock tower. It isn't as big as Big Ben. Our village has only about eighty inhabitants, so Small Ben suits us well enough. Friends who come for the weekend wake up in the night and hear a clock chiming. Then they hear another one. Next day they ask me 'Where's the other clock? We can see one up there above the church but we've walked all round and we can't see the one that's a bit slow.' Well, it's the same clock. There's only one. We're in the Midi, the south of France – the unfashionable end. Down here the clocks tell you the hour twice. That's a very good idea, because when there are a lot of strokes, say after six o'clock, you get another chance to count them.

When Sophie and I moved in here it took us a while to get used to the village clock. Midnight is quite a thing, with no fewer than forty strokes. There are the 'Westminster' chimes – bong ting clang bong, four times. That makes sixteen strokes. Then the twelve for midnight, and then a minute later another twelve. After that we used to stay awake, wondering if we would go to sleep before the four chimes of a quarter past twelve. However, after a week or so we got adjusted; and now, on the rare occasions when the clock stops working, we don't sleep quite so well. Our unconscious minds need those chimes to tell us that it isn't time to wake up yet.

I'm very grateful to that clock. It helped me get integrated into village life. It's important to get integrated if you want to settle happily in a small village. The first step is to reassure people that you're a human being and not, for example, the sort of Parisian who rents one of the holiday cottages, wanders around the streets in bathing trunks and says the inhabitants are lazy because he doesn't see them at work in their vineyards. Well, they were there at half-past five in the morning in the cool, while he was fast asleep. What about the British? You don't need to speak more than two or three words of French. If you come in a posh car and you and your family spend all day every day on the beach, half an hour's drive away, that's all right. But if you don't say *'Bonjour Madame'* every time you pass old Madame Roques, who sits most of the time on a bench in the square just outside your house, you aren't integrated at all. They won't be rude: they'll look at you politely, but rather carefully, as if perhaps you were extraterrestrials of uncertain habits. People do like to be able to place people.

We were lucky. We moved in fifteen years ago on 10 November. The eleventh is a public holiday in France. When we lived in England we never went on parade on Remembrance Day. It's not the sort of thing we were keen on and I had quite enough of going on parade in the war. But we thought we'd go along this time and see what happened. After all, we were allies.

At eleven o'clock all the eighty or so inhabitants of our village assemble in the square, and then straggle along to the war memorial in the cemetery. A wreath is laid and the youngest child who can read does the roll call. There are twelve names from the First World War, and four from the Second. And of course those are the family names of our neighbours. So it goes like this: 'Jacques Estelle . . .' and everyone choruses *'Mort pour la France'*. 'Paul Estelle . . .' *'Mort pour la France'*. And by the time we reach the ninth or tenth name it's really quite moving. Then there's a minute's silence. The Mayor makes a very short conventional speech, and we all troop down to the village hall. Aperitifs and soft drinks are waiting. All that's on the rates, by the way. Then the Mayor makes another speech, a longer one this time. It's not about the war, but about the events of the past year. Births, marriages and deaths; who's come, who's gone, and what the village council is up to.

So on our first 11 November we met everybody. And they seemed to regard us as fairly normal. Harmless, anyway, if given the benefit of the doubt, and properly brought up in the matter of shaking hands – a thing one has to do all day long in France.

A few days later Sophie and I were sitting in our garden in the sun, out of the shadow of the clock tower. Suddenly we heard the creak of a massive door, and a few moments later there was the noise of ratchets clicking overhead. We could see that something was going on behind the slats of a window up at the top of the tower. I went out into the street, through our garden gate, and saw that the door at the bottom of the tower was unlocked. I should

have told you that the church and its separate bell-tower form one wall of our garden. Perhaps long ago our house was the vicarage, as it were. (Nowadays a leather-jacketed young priest turns up on his motor-bike from a bigger village.) I plucked up my courage, went into the tower, up the spiral staircase and up an iron ladder, and found Henri Poujol winding the clock.

It's a lovely bit of nineteenth-century machinery. There are cogwheels two feet in diameter, pinions and ratchets and damping vanes and levers and sproozling-irons and nurdling-rods; and there are chains and wires going up through the roof to swing the hammers of the five bells that hang up there in the open, under the weathercock. Five bells – that's four for the Westminster chimes and a bigger one for the hours. Other villages have electric clocks; so, when a gale blows the power lines down or lightning strikes some vital part – and that sort of thing does sometimes happen down here – the clocks in the other villages stop dead. But not ours. We're ecological. There are three mighty weights, and if you wind them right up to the top you've got ten days before they touch bottom again. The smallest weighs about a hundredweight. That turns the hands. Two bigger ones work the Westminster chimes and the hours. Henri let me wind up one of them with the great starting handle. And afterwards we had a drink and a gossip together in the garden. One thing led to another, and I ended up by volunteering to take on the clock. If you can't beat 'em, join 'em.

Henri has quite a lot on his plate. He does all the work on his twenty-five acres of vineyards, except when the

Spaniards and the students come for the vintage, as well as the paperwork of this commune of eighty inhabitants. In France they like six copies of everything, usually with a passport photograph on each. In England you go to the Registrar of Births, Marriages and Deaths, or you go to the Town Hall, or you go to see the County Council or perhaps the Land Registry, or maybe it's the DSS, or the Passport Office. In a French village most of it's done at the Mairie. And our Mairie is open every evening, with Henri – who is the Secretary – and the Mayor on duty. So it's not really surprising that Henri appointed me Deputy Acting Unpaid Clock-Winder and handed over the great key of the tower. I have the sole right of entry to this edifice and I'm proud of it. If there's another Englishman in the Midi with similar rights and duties, I hope he'll show up. We'll have a contest, and may the fastest winder win.

The great thing was, it gave me a satisfactory label. Writing, and things like that, are lonely and mysterious activities. But you know where you are with the Englishman who winds the clock.

It's nice up in my engine-room. The daylight filters through the clock-face, which is about six feet in diameter and made of glass painted white. A bulb behind the face comes on at dark, so it shines like the full moon. To adjust the time you have to learn to read it back to front. No one's ever been able to synchronise the audio and the visual; there's a three-minute gap between the clock-face and the chimes. But we're not obsessional about that sort of thing down here. When twelve strikes we know it's about three minutes to, if the clock's right – which it usually is, give or take five minutes.

Then if I go up another ladder, I'm on the roof under

the bells. They hang from a wrought-iron framework, up in the air. I can see for miles. There's a far-distant gleam from the Mediterranean. It's beyond the great plain, which has millions of gallons of plonk on the vines. And, looking the other way, there are the hills of the garrigue with their scented shrubs and dwarf oaks and those prickly plants with sticky sap that survive the drought and the hungry sheep.

And there's Monsieur Planas, the travelling grocer, hooting his way along the lanes towards the village. And there's Madame Combadazou. She's getting a nice suntan on her private terrace, hidden from every eye but mine. Peeping Tom? No, I feel more like a minor god. I've got a lovely world.

But nothing is perfect, though, in any world. One evening last winter we came back from a couple of days in Paris. As we turned into the village square five o'clock started to chime. One, two – and then silence. I was stricken with guilt. I rushed to the tower, unlocked the door – but no, the weights were half-way up. I ran up the stairs, shot up the ladder. In the twilight, puffing a bit, I inspected the machinery, with its sad motionless pendulum. I poked and jogged and gave it a kick or two. Total defeat.

So I was at the Mairie as soon as Henri Poujol got there for his evening secretarial duties. We waited for the Mayor to finish his day's work in the vineyards. We all went up the tower again, failed to diagnose the disease, and decided that we should have to call in the specialist from Montpellier, thirty miles away. That would mean probably waiting a week or so. Humiliating.

But next morning, just for something to do, I went

sadly up the tower again. And I noticed something in the brighter light. Sticking out from where a big wheel meshes with a small cog was a postage-stamp-sized bit of what looked like red and black shot silk. It was the wing of a butterfly. The butterfly must have carelessly settled there. And then, at five, the monstrous machine started turning . . .

There must be a moral to this somehow, but I can't think what.

MADAME JULIE

Madame Julie was the first person we met in this village. It seems a long time ago. In the morning the estate agent had driven us along the winding lanes and shown us the house. My wife Sophie thought it would do, as a house, but what about the village? So that afternoon we came back by ourselves to make a reconnaissance. The house is on the village square, and in the square there's a bench under a mulberry tree, and on the bench was a witch. She was small, very aged, and dressed in black except for her apron. She was stroking a wicked-looking Siamese cat and she had a thin straggly white beard. Several months later, when we moved in, we found out that she kept a tame owl in her kitchen. It was a scops owl, *Otus Scops*, a small sort that just goes 'Oop' instead of 'Tu-whit-tu-whoo' like a proper English owl. You don't get them up in the Frozen North. We were friends with her by then, and one day – on the lines of 'Good morning, Sergeant-Major, here's a sparrow for your cat' – we brought her a mouse that we had caught in the cellar. But she said no, she always fed her owl on steak. Her aristocratic Siamese turned its nose up too. Never

17

mind, it's the thought that matters. Madame Julie would have had to be careful if she'd lived a few hundred years ago in witch-hunting country.

That first afternoon we plucked up our courage and approached the bench. Sophie made an admiring remark about the cat, who spat. I said *'Bonjour Madame*. We are wondering about buying that empty house opposite. What would be the reaction here if a couple of English people settled in?'

'No need to worry', she said. 'No one minds foreigners here. Why, the Mayor's a foreigner. He comes from somewhere near Millau.'

Now Millau is all of fifty miles away, northwards, in the Aveyron. A different sort of country, admittedly. Here it's vineyards, but up there it's all wild moors where sheep and shepherds roam. The sheep are there to be milked and the milk is made into cheese at Roquefort.

We were pleased to learn that English people wouldn't necessarily be regarded as any more alarming than people from up there. Soon afterwards two more old ladies came to reinforce Madame Julie on the bench. Yes, we had two children; but no, they wouldn't be coming because they were grown up and established in London. That seemed to be a pity. We gathered that there was a village primary school, but it had only eight pupils, and there was a risk of its being closed if the numbers went down. We were sorry we couldn't oblige; well, I suppose we *could* have done, just – we were in our mid-forties then – but keeping the birth rate going wasn't on our agenda that afternoon.

We had put a toe in the water and found it warmish.

People didn't seem to want to see a house remain empty on the village square. Moving into a village isn't like moving into a block of flats in a town. It's more like coming to occupy vacant seats at a table in a restaurant. We felt that if Madame Julie and her friends didn't mind, it would be all right. Then it was time for the Siamese cat to have his afternoon cup of *café au lait* and we said *au revoir* for the next three months.

After we moved in we got to know her better. We soon discovered that she held an official position. She was the town crier. She went around the narrow streets and the square blowing a trumpet and calling out *'Avis à la population!* The water will be cut off this afternoon between two o'clock and four o'clock!' or *'Avis à la population!* A new fishmonger has arrived on the square with a wide selection of fish!'

There's usually a glut of peaches round here in the season, and she was good at making peach jam. She used to give us a pot from time to time, especially if I had given her a lift from the bus stop on a Wednesday. That's market day in our nearest town, four miles away. It's a good market and the village housewives all used to like to go there. They still do, even though the town now has a monster hypermarket with a car park and trolleys, because at the real market you meet all your friends from other villages and you can have a nice talk. The bus stop on the road is only a quarter of a mile from the square, and the avenue of plane trees shades you from the sun; but it's uphill, and in the summer when the cicadas are squeaking their hot-weather song it's a bit tiring if you're a very old lady lugging two heavy string bags. And she liked to get home early to make a good lunch for Zézé. Zézé was her son. He was a bachelor, knocking on sixty, working in the vineyards. She lived with Zézé and her cat and – for a short time – her owl, which she had rescued when its wing was injured somehow. She had had a daughter, who died at the age of twelve, long before the war. Her husband had died in 1950.

We had a short chat with her almost every afternoon because that was when she went and sat on the bench with her friends. They say that the French aren't sociable. That isn't true, at any rate in the south. But they're great respecters of privacy. They don't pop into one another's houses, drinking casual cups of tea and borrowing half a pound of sugar. They need a neutral place in which to socialise, and one of the places in our village is the bench in the square. It's one of those metal affairs painted green, with round holes just the right size to jam an old centime piece in, if you can find one. And it's light enough for two old ladies to move it around. It has a complex orbit according to the time of day and the time of year, keeping in the sun in the winter and following the shade in the summer, with variations according to the wind. Sophie used to chat with Madame Julie there sometimes, learning useful things like when to get your hair cut. If it's getting thin and you want to encourage vigorous growth, get it cut in the first or second quarter of the moon. But if you're mean, like me, and don't want to go to the barber's too often, go at the old moon. The same goes for the garden. If you want leaves and stems, in the case of lettuces for instance, plant in the new moon. But if you want things to produce fruit and seeds – peas, beans, tomatoes, aubergines – plant them in the old moon. And there were her recipes, some dating from long ago and only for use in wartime when the rationing system breaks down: fox, for example. It might come in handy one day. Skin and gut your fox and suspend him in running water for forty-eight hours. Then marinate him in wine for twenty-four hours, and after that you can cook him in any of the ways you would use for a rather tough squirrel.

Madame Julie couldn't see very well, but she took part in all the village events. Good heavens, you'll be saying, do they have events in your one horse village? Oh yes, Knightsbridge or Tooting have nothing on us. Every Tuesday and every Saturday Rancoul the butcher and Planas the grocer come in their vans, hooting for the last kilometre, and install themselves in the square for an hour or two. And, even though they go to market on Wednesdays, the village ladies turn up. It's another occasion for a meeting. And Planas is a splendid source of news and gossip. He circulates throughout the week around twenty villages, all too small to have a shop. He knows everybody, he passes on messages and (unlike the discreet local paper) he has astounding revelations.

Then there's the village excursion. It takes place in June, when there's not so much to do in the vineyards. We go in a hired coach. Sophie sat near Madame Julie and Zézé the first year we were here, and learnt a lot: local history, geography, sociology and biography, especially biography. The coach started from the square at four in the morning. We stopped for breakfast at Valence. There was a pause at Grenoble, for everyone to have a trip up and down the hill on the town's cable railway. Then we

went up into the Vercors. That's a high mountain plateau, the scene of a tragic stand by the resistance in the war. We saw the remains of the gliders that the SS came in, to wipe out the Maquis; and the military cemetery, which also has civilian graves because the SS shot everyone they suspected. The whole family Blanc is there, in a neat row of graves, from Grandmother Blanc, aged eighty, to the baby, aged eighteen months. It's a moving place, up there among the mountain peaks, with the red, white and blue flag fluttering under the clouds. Then down the hairpin bends to the plain, to go round the winery where they make the Clairette de Die, a sparkling white wine a quarter of the price of champagne. And all sixty of us – that's three-quarters of the village – had dinner at a restaurant at Bagnols. After that, going home in the coach, there was some singing. Madame Julie taught us the words of *La Pêche aux Moules* and of *Coupo Santo*. That one isn't in French; it's in the local patois, which is a close relation of Catalan and Provençal. We got back to the village at a quarter to one in the morning, full of life. The excursion is always on Saturday, because people who aren't real villagers do sometimes feel a little tired the next day.

Then there's the village open-air dinner on the Fourteenth of July. The main dish is usually a *brasucado* of rabbit. The Mayor and his helpers make a great fire of vine twigs pruned off in the winter. When it's all reduced to glowing embers they put down a grid, six feet long by three feet wide, and the rabbits go on that. Most people lend a hand in the preparations. In our first year they decided, after some hesitation, that Sophie and I could be trusted to hard-boil eighty eggs. Madame Julie had the trickier responsibility of making the great bowls of mayonnaise.

Then there was the night of terror. It was a bingo night. Oh yes, we play bingo. It's called *loto*. It's strictly controlled by law. Each commune can hold three *loto* nights, the proceeds to be devoted to local good causes. The prizes have to be provisions. In big communes they rise to whole mutton carcasses to go in the deep-freeze, but turkeys are our limit. While it was going on (*soixante-dix-neuf – hein? – setanta-nou* – that's the patois – *eh? – seventy-nine* – that's me, nudging our son Arthur who is over for a winter break) the rumour went round that cat-catchers were scheduled to come in a van from the town in the early morning to round up all the wild cats and put them in the pound for two days. If any were in fact tame cats, their owners would claim them; and the rest would . . . disappear. There were a score of these cats. Not really wild, just hippies. Marginals, the French call such beings when they're human. They slept rough, near one of the big swing-lid bins that we put our rubbish into. Each of these marginal cats had a favourite old lady who would bring it delicious offerings every day, and be rewarded with a purr and a rub around the shins with a vertical tail.

As soon as the last prize had been won there was a midnight rush to the rubbish-bin and plaintive cries of 'Minou, Minou!' Sophie's little friend spent an agitated night in the garage. The council got only five last-ditch independents. Madame Julie proudly announced that she had sheltered three in her cellar – not in the house, of course, the Siamese wouldn't have liked it. And two of these were pregnant, she was happy to say.

The end of Madame Julie's story came rather quickly. Zézé had a sore throat and difficulty in swallowing. Madame Julie told us: 'Good news! The specialist isn't going to operate; there's some sort of treatment.' So twice a week Zézé went off thirty miles to the big teaching hospital in Montpellier. Madame Julie's doctor had been trying for a long time to get her to have an operation to restore her eyesight. She had always refused. She knew her way around, she could see quite a bit, and she wasn't a nuisance. In our little village everybody keeps an eye on everybody else. That's inhibiting for the young, but convenient for the elderly and the infirm. Anyway, Zézé and the doctor talked Madame Julie round at last. The operation was a success. She could see much better. From the eye clinic, though, she went to the old people's ward in the town where she used to go to the market on Wednesdays. It's a bit of a shock, an operation like that and all the assorted goings-on. She hadn't exactly gone gaga . . . but she wasn't quite herself. She came back to the village some afternoons, when someone fetched her in a car. The Siamese disappeared, perhaps looking for its *café au lait* elsewhere. The owl had flown away long ago. Zézé was permanently in hospital. And then he died.

We went and saw her in the old people's ward. 'Oh no!' she said. 'I never thought they'd all go before me! Oh no! Oh no!'

She soon went. You can see the dates of birth of her husband, her daughter and her son on the graves in the village cemetery, but it seems no one will ever know how old Madame Julie was.

WORK, STATISTICS AND
ALL THAT

Our village looks its best from the top of the church tower because you can see the roofs. There are some little modern villas on the outskirts but the bulk of the village lies below, a Picasso-like surface of irregular planes. The streets don't break it up noticeably because they're so narrow. This surface is made of what are called Roman tiles, invented when Ancient Rome was young. They are tapering half-cylinders, if you don't object to the idea of a tapering cylinder. They rest without any fixing except at the edges of each roof. Of course the slope of the roof has to be shallow, but that's all right: we never get snow here. The rain falls in great bucketfuls and then goes away again for two or three months.

When they're new, these tiles are plain orange-red. It's when they've matured that they become interesting. After a hundred years or more, the baking sun and various accidents – birds, lichen, cats – turn them all colours: ham omelette, aubergine, cornflakes, spaghetti bolognese, lobster, even egg on spinach, all nicely mixed up because of renewals and replacements. They're cheap to make, but a roof of old ones can be sold for a lot of money and end up on a millionaire's pad at St Tropez. There's a new roof of horrid pink modern tiles just below. It belongs to a family from Lille, up in the North. Their rafters needed replacing and they partly paid for the job by selling the old tiles. They're only here on holidays, so they didn't hear the nasty things we all said when the merchant took those beautiful vintage tiles away in his lorry.

I said we never get snow down here. That's because I'm quoting statistics. Statistics are made by adding things up and then dividing them by the number you first thought of. One day far too hot and one day far too cold produces a delightful average temperature.

In fact, there's been snow five times in the fifteen years Sophie and I have been here. That works out at nought-point-three-recurring times a year – which, to the nearest whole number, is indeed zero. But in January 1987 we had a blizzard and several cubic feet of the white stuff shot sideways under all the north-facing Roman tiles. Luckily the temperature was well below freezing so it didn't melt until a week later, by which time the electricity had come on again. It took a long time for the snow under the tiles to melt. We put buckets and baths to catch the drips in our upstairs rooms, and I calculated that I caught over a hundred gallons. In the house opposite a wet ceiling and a cubic metre of slush fell on the bed, fortunately when Monsieur and Madame Combadazou weren't in it. However, the temperature didn't drop to freezing point again until December 1990. Nearly four years! So the statistics can still say 'no snow, no frost', and I still like those semi-cylindrical nearly-horizontal Roman tiles.

What part do the people under those roofs play as a statistic in generating the Gross National Product? It's summer now, so about a quarter of the village houses are filled with summer people. Sophie and I were the first foreigners, but we're here all the year round. The holiday houses have been bought by people from Paris and Lille; and there's a London family, a Rotterdam family and a Kaiserslautern family. They come down when they can. And some of the houses are let furnished, by the fortnight, to holidaymakers. If we leave them out, and the retired, everybody works. Only three people have jobs outside the village. The rest grow grapes to make wine.

I expect you know all about wine. The British win all the wine-tasting contests, and sometimes our Masters of Wine pop up on French TV to explain the finer points to the natives. But let's get it into perspective. France produces about 75 million hectolitres of wine per year. That's 1650 million gallons, or enough to fill 10000 million standard wine bottles. About one per cent of that is what the Masters of Wine go on about. Most of the other ninety-nine per cent is produced down our way. It sounds a lot, but there are 55 million people in France. Ten thousand million bottles is 182 bottles a head, or only half a bottle a day. I hope you appreciate how kind we are to export a little to the UK. Fifty pence a litre it costs me, when I fill up my jerrycans at the local *cave coopérative*, and it's worth every penny. It's decent honest plonk, nothing to write poetry about but noticeably better – and cheaper – than the stuff I used to make in the airing-cupboard back in Cornwall with cans of concentrated grape juice from the chemist.

People who come down here in the summer for the first time think that the locals have it easy. It's true that there's not a lot to do in July except to take out the tractor half an hour before dawn and get in four hours' spraying in the cool, before the summer people think of going down to the lake for a swim. And then you wait for the grapes to ripen. 'What do they do in the winter?' you ask. 'Make cuckoo clocks?' The answer is: they prune. The average holding is about twenty-five acres, just enough in an average year to support a family and two tractors (one small, to go between the rows, and a big one on stilts that can straddle two rows). Grapes grow on the new wood of the year: seven or eight branches that sprout from a knobbly stump three feet high. After the grape harvest all those branches have to be cut off, leaving carefully chosen 'eyes' for the next year's branches.

Twenty-five acres is about 40 000 stumps to be pruned. Prune them in five winter months: that's 8000 a month, or 260 a day, or a minute and a half per stump in an eight-hour day. You can get tennis elbow and golf wrist doing that. Henri Poujol uses pneumatic secateurs, with a little two-stroke engine puttering at the end of the row and a rubber tube going to his secateurs. Jacques Delmas, the Mayor, has gone electric with a couple of accumulators strapped to his waist. Others stick to old-fashioned muscle power, but they bully their children into helping out.

So in winter the vineyard owners are dotted around, one every twenty-five acres, wearing balaclava helmets and mittens if the north wind is blowing. Sometimes there's a plume of smoke: an oil-drum cut in half length-

ways, mounted on a pair of wheels rescued from the dump, makes a good brazier for burning some of the pruned branches and thawing numb fingers.

Then there's hoeing by tractor and spraying by tractor. You spray against weeds, black rot, red spider, *l'oïdium*, *le mildiou* and half a dozen other menaces. And you need to find time occasionally to root out old vines with a massive plough that goes down four feet, with people sitting on it for extra weight. Vines have tremendously deep roots. Then you plant superior varieties that give less juice per acre but higher quality, because people in France are drinking less plonk nowadays; they want *appellation contrôlée*.

The grape harvest, the vintage, takes about three weeks starting in mid-September. In the old days labour was cheap. Whole families used to trek down from the mountains of the Cévennes. Many hands meant enough leisure for the romantic picture: guitar-playing and snogging under the harvest moon. Then the French got richer and so train-loads of Spaniards used to come, bringing their bacon and beans, and working twelve hours a day to make enough cash to tide them over the winter. Then the Spaniards got rich too. Nowadays Spanish children wear shoes, go to school, and see the doctor when they need to – at least, the Spaniards in Catalonia, near the border. A few still come from Extremadura, right on the other side, but on the whole machines are taking over. Driving a grape-picking machine isn't so sociable and not romantic at all.

For fine wines they still use people, at a minimum wage of about four pounds an hour, and employers' social security charges that add fifty per cent to that. But, as I said, we don't make that sort of wine down here.

Off go the grapes in lorries to the co-operative winery. They're dumped down chutes, a different chute for each variety, a computer weighs the juice and registers the sugar content and clocks it up, and there's your income for the next year. I may have made it sound dull. But it seems a healthy life and Henri Poujol and Jacques Delmas are firmly convinced that growing grapes is what man was put on earth for. After all, the first thing Noah did when the mud dried and he'd sent all those smelly animals out of the way was to plant a vineyard.

And then the village helps to provide a living for other people. Look, there's Paul Planas, the grocer, driving his van into the village square. All the old ladies are coming out. They love his twice-weekly performance. He's a bouncy little man. He teases them without going too far, bursts into song and brings them news from the other villages on his round. I called on him one evening to learn about his trade. I asked him if he envied salaried workers who do thirty-nine hours a week. He said: 'What I envy is their five weeks' holiday. I take a week a year. You can't take more in my job. Customers can lay in a week's provisions, but no more. The point is, I like being my own boss. I do an eighty-hour week. I go round all the little villages near here, and I suppose I know everyone: their names and their nicknames, their politics, who are their friends and whom they don't speak to, whether they're on a diet, the name of their dog and the name of their cat. I'm up at half-past five every morning, and I do my round five days a week. Wednesday is market day in the town, and people go there by bus or in their cars, so that's the day I go to lay in my stock at the wholesalers. Of course most people have got cars nowadays, and there are supermarkets in the town. But I've still got my customers. What the people without cars would do without me, I don't know. It's true though: the grandmothers outnumber the grand-daughters. Grand-daughters go away. Of course there are risks. One day last year I delivered a box of groceries to an old lady. She said "Mind the stairs," but I didn't. I rolled down and cracked four ribs. The doctor said, "I'll give you a fortnight off duty". "No you won't" I said. "I can't stop working". So I carried on. When a convict comes out of prison he gets unemployment benefit, but if I'm ill I get nothing. I'm not complaining, though. I like to keep going.'

He certainly does. Two evenings a week he helps train the market town's junior rugby team, and two more evenings he rehearses with the brass band. He plays a good loud trumpet. Long may he continue! His father did the job before him, but Planas has ambitions to get his son, who is ten at the moment, into the Post Office. Job security, five weeks' holiday . . . What will the twenty little villages on his round do when Planas retires? The old people will have to give shopping lists to the car-owners, I suppose. No more cheerful gossipy gatherings in the square on Tuesday and Saturday mornings. Still, he's only forty. We should be all right until 2015.

Ah, there's Dr Tessier's car coming up the avenue of plane trees. I wonder whom he's going to see? We shall soon know, of course. That's what living in a little village in the Midi is like. You need to tell people what's up, or they worry.

Dr Tessier comes from a village two miles away, and he's only got a Renault 5. Village allegiance is split between him and Dr Chazottes, who comes from the market town four miles away and has a Mercedes. These two doctors have different approaches to disease, or rather to patients. I ought to explain that the French National Health system works differently from the British one. You pay the doctor and the chemist in cash, and then you send off a form and get three-quarters of your money back, or more if you've got something really nasty and long-lasting. Now there are a lot more doctors in France than in England. So there's quite stiff competition to get patients. Dr Tessier, the one with the small car, is the one we usually choose, though we have tried Dr Chazottes. You aren't registered with a doctor in France; you can shop around as you fancy. If you get 'flu, Dr Tessier will probably prescribe aspirins, freshly squeezed orange juice and keeping warm. Dr Chazottes, on the other hand, is likely to fling in antibiotics, aerosol inhalers, nicely flavoured fizzy vitamin pills and some big suppositories for your headache. Suppositories for headache, you ask? Oh yes, it's very logical, and the French take their stomachs seriously. If the main ingredient is absorbed into the system in the large intestine it might as well go in there straight away, instead of taking the long way round via the duodenum and all that. When Dr Tessier's patient goes to the chemist he doesn't pay much for his aspirin, and of course he doesn't get much back from the National Health apart from three-quarters of the cost of Dr Tessier's visit. But Dr Chazottes' patient counts out a wad of banknotes to the chemist, and then three weeks later he gets a large and satisfying sum back. Quite worth being ill, really, with Dr Chazottes – you get full value for your Social Security contributions. That, I think, is why the French are the world's champion consumers of expensive medicines, and why Chazottes runs a Mercedes. Never mind, the French live a little longer than the English on average. As for our last two deaths, Monsieur Mazel was Dr Tessier's patient and he died at eighty-five, bang, just like that, after a morning's gardening, as he was starting his dinner. Madame Espinasse had Dr Chazottes. She only reached seventy-nine, but her last six months were dramatically occupied in keeping up with the latest marvels of medical science and getting great big refunds from the Social Security office.

As for my contribution to village income, well, I write and everybody knows that isn't work. I think I'll have a little stroll now and see how the grapes are getting on.

PROGRESS IN THE MIDI

Progress marches on. Electricity came to this little village in southern France in the last century and we wouldn't want to be without it. Last winter the current was off for a whole day because a gale blew some power lines down. Old Madame Roques, who lives next door, complained that she couldn't make any coffee for breakfast because there wasn't any light. And Monsieur Combadazou, opposite in the square, said he couldn't shave for the same reason. It seemed odd to me, because it was a clear bright day with the sky as blue as a Gauloise packet – that official French blue you see everywhere. When a gale blows it chases the clouds away over the Mediterranean. Then I learnt a bit more French. Electricity is now cheap, cheaper than in England, but before the war it used to be expensive. The only things people ran off it in those days were electric light bulbs. And so older people still call electricity *la lumière*, the light. Madame Roques' coffee grinder and Monsieur Combadazou's razor are not powered by ecological photo-electric cells or solar panels, like the Mayor's water heater. They're just electric, they work off *la lumière* and to get *la lumière* you have to flip a switch. Luckily by supper time the linesmen got the supply of light flowing again down the wires.

And some time before the last war the village had real drains and piped water. As for unpiped water, the village has been sitting pretty since pre-Roman times because of our splendid spring. In fact the spring is why the village is here. There are other villages around which had enough water in the old days, but now they've got washing machines and flush loos and even bath-tubs, so you can see why they have a water crisis when the summer people come from Paris and Lille and Hamburg and Chipping Sodbury. But we're all right, Jacques!

Way back in time the spring must have welled up in a rocky pool down at the bottom of the village, and people would have gone there to fill water-jars and buckets. Long before the war the pool was concreted over and there's a pump – yes, it works by light – in a concrete sentry-box on top. It switches itself on in the evening and sends water uphill in a pipe to fill a concrete reservoir hidden in a wood of pine trees. Three or four hours' pumping is enough to fill the reservoir with all the water we need. It's good water, rather hard because of all the limestone, but bacteriologically pure according to the analyses you can read every quarter on the village notice board outside the Mairie. For the rest of the twenty-four hours the water flows into the *lavoir*. That's a row of eight stone troughs, holding about 100 gallons each, with a useful ledge for bashing clothes on. Nobody does an entire wash there now, because everybody has a machine. But quite a few houseproud housepersons think there's nothing like a good final rinse in unlimited quantities of clear spring water. It's no great hardship – the water seems lukewarm in winter and nicely cool in summer. Then they hang out their sheets on the municipal washing lines, next to the *lavoir*. These days sheets tend to be pink or blue or even paisley-patterned, and it makes a fine sight when they're all flapping in the breeze. Once a sheet was stolen, and they're still talking about it. That was in 1957, before we came. Luckily we're not on the road to anywhere; any strange car that stops near the washing lines would be the subject of a lot of interested comment.

And then, after the *lavoir*, the water from the spring flows on downhill to fill another reservoir in the middle of the allotments. Some of the owners or tenants of these allotments come from six or seven miles away to do their gardening, because a garden that you can water is a valuable prize in the Midi. We get about the same annual rainfall as London, but it tends to arrive in short violent downpours in autumn or spring. Summer tourists see road signs: INTERDIT PAR SUBMERSION – no entry when under water – on some of the roads down here. If they stop and look around they see they're on a little bridge over a gully. Ten feet below there's a stream-bed, bone dry or with a tiny trickle of water. They think we're exaggerating, as people in the Midi are supposed to do. But when there's a *gros orage* – a proper rainstorm – the stream fills up and there are floods and minor landslides. However, from May to September it's dry down here. That suits the grapes in the vineyards. You don't want too much water in the wine.

But tomatoes and aubergines and melons need watering twice a week. So you open a little sluice in the dam by

the allotments, and the water flows down a channel. You block that channel at the right place, with a plastic bag filled with earth, to send the water through your particular hole into your allotment. Then you have to do some quick work with a heavy hoe to make it run into the irrigation channels you've made among your vegetable beds. Homer's Odysseus was washed ashore near the vegetable gardens of King Alcinous, the father of the lovely Nausicaa, and it was the same system in those days. Plant your lettuces too low down in the channel you've made and they drown. Plant them too high up the ridge and they die of thirst. It's trickier than it sounds. It took me quite a while to learn, because of course back in Cornwall if there hasn't been a shower for a week it's a drought, and I was used to wandering about scattering gentle droplets with a hose. Down here my gardening neighbours were helpful, showing me how to dig my trenches and ridges so that the water would fill them efficiently. At first I felt that one couldn't possibly garden without a spirit-level because it's not easy to avoid going imperceptibly uphill, with the result that the channel stays bone dry and dusty, or a tiny bit downhill, so that the seeds float up in the middle of a mud puddle. All that helped me to get integrated.

Allotment holders are notoriously competitive anywhere in the world, but I was no competition. My fellow gardeners – especially Jordi, who has the allotment next to mine, and I'll be telling you about him in a minute – grasped that I was handicapped by my unfortunate upbringing somewhere in the Frozen North. But when I showed that I didn't need telling more than two or three times how to do it, they seemed to think I was well on the way to becoming a normal human being.

Yes, well, there hasn't been any progress since the *Odyssey* in the matter of watering by irrigation, and I can't see the gardeners clubbing together to build a separate water tower with its own pump so that they can use hoses. As far as they're concerned messing about with little canals like children on a beach is the proper way to do it.

As for my friend Jordi, is he the victim of progress? I'm sure he doesn't think so, because he's just retired at over seventy. He could have retired much earlier, but he kept on because of Bijou. Bijou is – no, was – the last horse. And Jordi has retired from the position of being the last of the farm labourers. In the late 1940s, I'm told, the vineyard owners in this village had thirty horses among them, and that meant thirty employees to look after them. Nowadays wages are higher, and there's social security. So no more employees. Specialised tractors, some up on long legs that can straddle the rows of grapes, get jobs done faster and cheaper than horses, each with its attendant man.

Bijou had become the last surviving horse years ago when we came to the village. In those days we used to work in London in the winter. The first time we came back here in May we went for a walk in the evening after we had unloaded the car. And there, in the sunset, against a background of cypresses and olive trees, was Bijou, coming down the path after his day's work: slow, white, dignified, enormous, with Jordi – a big, handsome man himself – riding him and singing a song in Catalan. He looked like a Roman, like an ancient Greek, like a

Visigoth. Or like a god. All right, it's a picture postcard scene, but it was so postcardy we felt like crying with joy.

I got Jordi's story while watering the tomatoes. He came from near Barcelona in Catalonia, and he was just old enough to fight against General Franco. When Franco won, Jordi and thousands of others crossed the border into the French part of Catalonia and were put into refugee camps. France fell and Pétain was going to send them all back, but Jordi escaped. He joined the resistance in the mountains of the Cévennes. After the war they gave him a medal and French citizenship. He got a job here, working in Monsieur Quatrefages' vineyards. As soon as he could he sent for his wife, whom he hadn't seen for eight years. They fitted in well, partly because they're nice people but also because Catalan is very like the local patois, which highbrows (but not the people who speak it) call Occitan. In Franco's time you could be arrested for speaking Catalan in Spanish Catalonia. There's no linguistic frontier. Catalan shades into Occitan, which shades into Provençal and then shades into Italian, going along from west to east. Oil is *aceite* in Spanish, but it's *oli* all the way from Barcelona until you get to Italy, where it's *olio*. All the older people in the village are bilingual. If I said 'A horse, a horse, my kingdom for a horse', only the young, who all do English at school, would understand a word. But 'Un cavall, un cavall, el meu reialme per un cavall' (yes, I bought a translation of *Richard III* in Figueras, just across the border in Catalonia) would be understood as easily as 'Un cheval, un cheval, mon royaume pour un cheval'. A few lines above in that play I see 'Per Sant Jordi!' – 'By Saint George'. Saint George or

Sant Jordi is the patron saint of both England and Catalonia. Anyway, what with speaking the patois already and being good with horses and a hard worker, Jordi was welcome. So was his family. His son did well at school. He is an aeronautical engineer in Toulouse now, making Airbuses.

Jordi paid us a great honour one hot spring day when we were sitting down for a break from cherry-picking. He rolled up a trouser leg, and then rolled up his long-john, and showed us where a bullet had gone through his knee. When the SS division Das Reich was on its way from here to Normandy he got his revenge with a Sten gun. (A remarkable British production that, very cheap to make. A Sten gun was dangerous at both ends, like a horse.)

As for horses, I prefer admiring them from a distance. Bijou was a fine animal, dappled grey in his youth. When we knew him he had turned a pleasing white. But I steered clear of his long yellow teeth – no sugar lumps from me, I'm afraid – and his great shaggy iron-clad hooves. Monsieur Quatrefages had five horses once (and of course five labourers to look after them) but Bijou was the sole survivor. There must have been a certain amount of sentiment there, or he wouldn't have kept him. You don't have to pay a horse but, unlike a tractor, his motor keeps running 365 days a year. Four or five gallons of oats a day, according to the mileage and how you drive, and I've forgotten how many hundredweight of hay per week. You have to buy that in the Midi: there aren't any hay-fields. No Social Security charges, but on the other hand the vet isn't on the National Health. Bijou was a bit of a luxury.

Bijou's stable was opposite Jordi's house, round the corner from us. Every morning at five Jordi's alarm went off. Bijou could hear it and if, twenty minutes later, Jordi wasn't around to give him his breakfast and a go with the brush, clonk! clonk! he used to go with his great feet against the door. We thought this proof of intelligence was charming. Jordi was more down to earth. Still, they got on well enough, Jordi and Bijou, like an old married couple. An arranged marriage, not a romantic one.

And then Bijou had his twenty-fifth birthday. Monsieur Quatrefages said that it really was time for Jordi to retire and sign on for the state Old Age Pension. What would happen to Bijou? we wondered. In Britain there are grassy homes for elderly horses, probably financed by legacies from people who prefer horses to any of their relations. But in France the Code Civil doesn't let you make that sort of will. So he shared the fate of Boxer, the carthorse in Orwell's *Animal Farm*, and went off to Montpellier. He weighed in at 750 kilos; three-quarters of a ton. The general opinion is that he will turn up on the supermarket shelves, in the shape of tinned pet food.

That's progress for you: from horses to tractors and poodles. Jordi has more time for his tomatoes and melons now. But he's sad that there's no more horse manure. He has to make do with a plastic sack of chemicals.

LA PLACE

What I'm talking about isn't really the village square, because it's got five sides and a couple of bits sticking out and none of the angles are right angles. It's the *Place*. Piccadilly Circus is a *Place* too, but ours is smaller. There are five ways in. One is a tunnel a yard wide under Monsieur Gal's house. Another is a flight of steps that leads to the *boulodrome*, which is a bumpy plot of earth half the size of a tennis court, where we play *boules* – or rather *pétanque*, that vigorous form of bowls where you fling iron balls around. Then there's a steep alley, which must have been useful in the days when they had donkeys. There are two sharp corners in it and it's wide enough for a moped to go down comfortably – and even to come up into the *Place*, if you like making a lot of noise. Our moped riders do, as a matter of fact. In France you can ride a moped when you're fourteen, which is what Master Delmas was last week. His moped doesn't go very fast or very reliably, but he modified the silencer so that it makes a most satisfactory noise as he comes up the alley. Slow but dramatic.

Then there's what you might call the main street. It

goes up the hill along the outside of the village and then doubles back through the houses to reach the *Place*. It's wide enough to let the vans of the visiting tradesmen – Rancoul the butcher and Planas the grocer – get into the *Place* twice a week. You can even get a furniture van through, with a certain amount of backing and the odd scratch. Young Delmas comes up the steep alley, crosses the *Place* like a machine-gun, up the narrow street below the church tower, round and down to the *boulodrome* and then back up the alley. About 500 yards, and it takes him two and a quarter minutes. I know because I've timed him. Not very fast, but inside his crash helmet he's on the Paris–Dakar rally, or chasing bandits in San Francisco.

The fifth way out is in front of our house. It's twenty yards long, and again it's just wide enough for a car. My garage is really the ground floor of the house, where a horse used to live. I come into the garage via the main street and the *Place*. I leave by backing out of the garage and going down through this shorter street. In effect it's a one-way street, because it's steep and has three shallow steps in it. It's all right for going down slowly – bump, bump, bump – but to come up it you would need a fair amount of momentum, which you can't have because at the bottom it's a T junction: left to get to the *boulodrome*, and right for the spring and the allotments. Young Delmas goes down it when he wants a change, but he would have to walk up, and walk is what he will not do since he reached moped age. Perhaps when he's old enough he will get a proper cross-country motor-bike, and then we shall see.

I've made it sound busy and dangerous, but it isn't. I

mean, you can hear young Delmas coming. Our village isn't on the road to anywhere. The only people who drive into the *Place* are people who make it their destination: mainly the grocer, the butcher, me and the terrorists. I'll tell you about them in a minute. There's a minor road that passes a quarter of a mile away. To get to us you have to leave that and come up a fine avenue of 200-year-old plane trees which doesn't take you anywhere else. Nobody passes through our village. If you're here it's because that's where you want to be. Quite different from Piccadilly Circus.

Now please don't think we're backward. The only vehicle in the *Place* at the moment is a pram under the mulberry tree, with the terrorists' baby in it, but there are thirty-two cars to our village – quite enough for the whole population to take off in if an emergency arose. Most of the cars are outside the central nucleus of the village. If you go up the church tower and look down you can see that it's a neat, defensive circle. Outside the circle there are ticky-tacky modern villas, built in the last twenty years. Most of the real permanent aboriginal inhabitants live in those. If I call them farmers it suggests cows and mangel-wurzels and that's quite different. What they are is *viticulteurs*, and my dictionary translates this as viticulturists, which doesn't help. They grow grapes for making wine, and they've been doing that since Roman times. Recently they've been getting advantageous loans from the Crédit Agricole to build smart modern villas. A few of them have sold off their old village houses – we bought one – but most keep them on, letting them furnished in the summer as holiday cottages. Like gold, house property is what people like to put their savings in – as well as vineyards of course.

Bits of the village might be a thousand years old, but it's not particularly beautiful. That is a good thing because if it were the kind of village people take pictures of it would be classified by the Ministry of whatever-it-is, and you wouldn't be allowed to paint your front door the colour you choose. When we first came, fifteen years ago, most of the façades were stucco, flaking off in patches. It gave an interesting weathered effect. Then there came a fashion for hacking the stucco off and exposing the big rough stones, and pointing the joints neatly with cement. At first it looks like a plastic imitation but it should be all right after twenty years or so. An even more popular fashion is to replace the stucco with ochre-coloured pebble-dash, just like the ticky-tacky villas. That's what they've done to the Mairie, behind the mulberry tree. But of course they've left the big label LIBERTÉ ÉGALITÉ FRATERИITÉ that runs all along the top. It's in multi-coloured mosaic and dates from the 1889 centenary of the Revolution, like the Eiffel Tower. A pity about the и. They did it the wrong way round in the next village too, but there it's carved in the stone and they were able to correct it with some more carving, so that their и has become an x with upright bars at each side. You can't do that with mosaic.

Next to the Mairie is Madame Jean's house. It's still got its peeling stucco because Madame Jean, who is of course a *viticulteur*'s widow, can't bear to destroy the climbing roses that cover the front of her house. Full marks to her, and may she live for ever.

Then comes the alley, and then the terrorists' house. It's small and was very dilapidated when they bought it a year ago; just a tap in the kitchen and that sort of thing. But they're both keen do-it-yourselfers and they've plumbed and wired and plastered, and covered the front with pebble-dash. Pink this time.

It took only a day or two to classify them as terrorists. They're a pale young couple from somewhere unknown in the North, perhaps even in those frozen regions beyond Paris. He's got an ear-ring and a beard, which is unusual in these parts because it's too hot for beards in the summer, though his beard doesn't look as though it would keep anyone very warm. And on the second day they were here she went out on the *Place* in bare feet – quite outlandish, that – to buy something from Planas the mobile grocer. When he recommended the very good ham he was slicing, she announced, and everyone could hear her, that they were vegetarians. Well, I ask you. That's the kind of thing that goes with weaving your own clothes, growing your own cannabis, and making your own bombs. And they didn't speak to anybody, not even *'bonjour'* to the old ladies who spend their afternoons knitting on the bench in the *Place*. And they left a dustbin outside their door, until the Mayor plucked up courage and dropped a hint. There are four swing-lid containers at strategic points around the village, and they're emptied twice a week, and that's where you put your rubbish. Oh no, we're not backward here.

Of course up in Paris, way back in the seventies when women who looked like the female terrorist were known as 'baba cool', there were flower children and marching ecologists. In the southern half of France, in the wild mountain regions, there were hippy groups with nanny-goats who tried to sell cheese to the motoring bourgeoisie, but they all went home to Amsterdam or Gelsenkirchen in the first hard winter. However, nobody like that had ever been in the village, and what got on the TV in the late eighties was the last hard core, the *Action Directe* gang, who were kind to animals but did a fair amount of murdering and blowing things up before they were captured.

Actually our couple are quite harmless. He has a desk job in town and goes there every day in his 2CV. They didn't speak to anybody because they're terribly shy. When she had a perfectly normal baby in perfectly normal conditions, and allowed the old ladies on the *Place* to coo at it, the verdict was 'not guilty'. But we still call them the terrorists. People do need a label.

Next to the terrorists' is Ernest Gal's house. He's a retired engine-driver, related in complex ways to four of our viticultural families. His wife has the Butagaz concession, so one goes to them when one's cylinder of bottled gas runs out. He was a prisoner of war in 1940, and they put him to work in a marshalling yard somewhere in Germany. One day he saw an empty wine-tanker on one of the sidings and he knew that eventually it would get back to the Midi to be re-filled with the local product. So he stole some rations and got in. The journey took three weeks and was pretty uncomfortable. He could only open the lid to get some fresh air at night when the train was moving, or he'd have been spotted. And when he got home he was ill for a month. He's got his escaped-prisoner-of-war certificate on the wall, and his label is 'the

senior Old Soldier'. He carries the flag on 11 November.

Then there's the main street, and then the church. It's plain and practical outside and, before we came, Vatican II had got rid of all the plaster statues, so that the inside is just austere whitewash – except for God the Centre-Forward, as the children call him. That's a big eighteenth-century polychrome wood carving, high up on the wall behind the altar. God has a blue football under his arm (I suppose it's the globe of the heavens) and he's raising his other hand in blessing, which looks as though he's acknowledging the cheers of the crowd. Theologically speaking this gives God a good image among the younger boys, though we're really in rugby country here.

Next to the church is us, and of course you know what our label is. I'm the Englishman and Sophie's the Englishwoman.

Being the Englishman has its ups and downs, usually connected with what's been on the telly. My stock went up three years ago, when Prince Charles was seen and heard to speak excellent French – a sure sign of high moral worth. After British football supporters have been on the box they eye me warily. *The Avengers* keeps turning up, dubbed into French, and Patrick MacNee is much admired. I haven't got a bowler hat, but I can whirl my umbrella. Sean Connery as James Bond is way beyond me, except when he's sitting down or walking slowly. Benny Hill in French is popular too, but I find him a nuisance. I keep explaining that Prince Charles is much more typical. And they showed the whole *Brideshead Revisited* series some while ago with Evelyn Waugh's characters all spouting French not quite in time with their jaw movements but being terribly, terribly English. The French TV people haven't bought *Coronation Street* or *EastEnders* . . . .

So I try to look like a mixture of Jeremy Irons, Patrick MacNee and Prince Charles, and then old Madame Roques says 'Oh Monsieur Areece, you do remind me of Bennee Eel.' Think of me, carrying the flag for you in one hand and the can in the other. Please be careful!

GETTING INTO THE MEDIA

*T*he power of the telly is extraordinary. Of course everyone in the village has a set whose size and elaborateness seem to vary in inverse proportion to its owner's academic status. Hard-working agriculturalists who don't exploit their knowledge of the three Rs further than reading the births-marriages-and-deaths in the local paper, and putting grains of maize on their bingo cards at the village *loto* sessions – they have colossal sets with video-recorders and quadraphonic sound, and they do their zapping by infra-red remote control. My neighbour Monsieur Bezombes has books in his house and gets by with a little set where you have to get up from your chair to switch off. They say that in a house in the woods, just outside the village, there's even a shameful black-and-white set. But the owner is only there for weekends and holidays – he's a professsor of Egyptology.

What I want to tell you about is how this village once got on the national TV. But first I have to explain about *Le Monde*. When you're used to *Le Monde* then *The Times* or the *Telegraph* seem like the *Beano* or the *Dandy*. I mean it doesn't descend to such vulgar things as news photographs, and although it does have headlines they tend to be in the form of sober sentences with verbs and punctuation. It's probably the best paper in the world if what you want is a background article, two pages long in small print, written by an expert about something that happened last week. It sells 400000 copies a day, which might be chicken-feed to Mr Murdoch or Lord Copper, but is really a tribute to the French, or perhaps Parisian, capacity for taking things seriously – from politics in Paraguay and Westminster to which restaurant in Paris can be trusted to do a *pot au feu* properly.

Ten years ago, not very long after Sophie and I came to live here, I did a series of short articles for *Le Monde*. That might surprise you – it certainly surprised me – because I'm not an expert in anything, and French isn't my mother tongue. But I don't let it frighten me. *Le Monde* had started a Sunday supplement – no, no, nothing like you have in England, just words with the occasional drawing – which was meant to be rather lighter than the usual stuff. After four years they dropped that idea, but it was nice while it lasted. My pieces were meant to be humorous: a British view of life in France. That was easy because, although the French, God bless them, are jolly good at weighty think-pieces and at rapier-sharp satire, they're a bit short on humour. In fact they think of it as a British speciality. What you and I call plain humour, they call *l'humour britannique*. So old British jokes are brand-new French ones. And then they're permanently fascinated by *les Anglais*, those strange people, so near and yet so far. There's a whole industry of writing about us, from Voltaire onwards, through André Maurois and his

Colonel Bramble down to Pierre Daninos and his Major Thompson. So there I was, ex-Sergeant Harris, less exalted but genuinely British, unlike that impostor Major Thompson, and cheap at the price and willing to tease them in the way they like to be teased.

Writing in French wasn't much of a problem either. The French find it very hard to write French – it's like drawing teeth to get a letter from the average Frenchman – because they learn the language entirely the wrong way, right from the start. They learn to *speak* it first, beginning in the cradle. Now when I was at school, before the war, there was no damn nonsense about speaking the lingo. The old School Cert. French exam had an oral as a minor optional extra, and boys who went in for it were thought of as rather unmanly. If anyone was going to go into the diplomatic service he'd wait till he'd finished with school and go and spend six months among the Frogs having private tuition at some establishment on the far side of the Channel. We did have one master who could speak French properly, but he suffered from the grave handicap of being a Frenchman. He was a small whiskery insanitary-looking specimen who never appeared on the sports field. We made his life hell. We had a song about him. 'Mr Manise' – that was his name – 'Mr Manise/The King of the fleas/Bought his wife a new chemise . . .' No, I'd better not go on. All the other masters were the real traditional stuff. If you could teach Latin or geometry you could teach French, with a stick of chalk, a cane and a book of grammatical exercises. Mr Downes got on with it. Was he a genuine sadist, or did he just get normal healthy enjoyment from wielding his cane five or six times a lesson? I don't know. I do know that the sounds he made were nothing like French as she is spoke, but thanks to him I have gone through life knowing more about the agreement of the past participle with the preceding direct object than ninety-five per cent of the population of France. At last I was able to use that information. Of course things are different nowadays in British schools. Teachers of modern languages can't say: 'Get on with exercise three on page ninety-six and I want to be able to hear a pin drop for the next half hour.' They spend their time messing about with tapes and wires in language laboratories, and their pupils make all the spelling mistakes the French make plus some sturdy home-grown ones.

What has this all to do with how we got on the telly? Well, every six years there are local elections in France. There are 36400 communes and each commune has a municipal council. Some communes are great big conurbations, with political parties and all that, and some are as small as our village – eighty inhabitants – or even smaller. Every six years most of our council gets re-elected, and we've had the same Mayor for ages. That's because Monsieur Delmas is good at his job. It's quite different from being an English mayor. In Delmas's case it's a proper part-time job, with a modest salary. As I've explained, the Mairie – which you might call the Town Hall – is on the village square opposite our house, and it's open every evening from half-past six until half-past eight when Delmas goes home to have his dinner. It's a long day for Delmas, because during the rest of the day he's a normal farmer, or rather vineyard owner, grape-grower and wine-maker. The Mayor is the equivalent of the Registrar of Births, Marriages and Deaths, the Town Clerk, the Planning Officer and the Citizen's Advice Bureau. Anyone who gets a form from anywhere goes to the Mairie first to have it explained. Delmas does all this and a lot more, helped by Henri Poujol, who acts as Secretary because in addition to running a vineyard he can type quite fast.

So the leading French television chain thought they would do a series of five-minute programmes after the main news, every evening for a week, showing what the work of a municipal council is like. They would end up with a big complicated town on Friday, but start on Monday with some tiny one-horse place in the sticks. Which one? The producer happened to have read some of my articles in *Le Monde*. She phoned me up. Did I think the Mayor and the council would co-operate, and would I contribute some observations on the differences between France and England in the matter of local government? I said no to the latter question, because I know next to nothing about either; but I promised to ask the Mayor what he thought, so long as the TV people would promise not to make fun of us. I ought to explain that we're as far from Paris as Aberdeen is from London and, while Londoners think that Highland villagers are pretty queer, living on haggises and bashed neeps, and dressed in sporrans and cairngorms, Parisians think that yokels in the Midi are even queerer. No, they said, they would respect us all deeply, and would I please ask the Mayor?

So I did. He called the council together. I told them that as far as I knew about such things, the electricians – as

Evelyn Waugh used to call them – would have us running up hill and down dale for a whole day or longer, and then perhaps all our unpaid efforts would be wasted because they might decide not to show the thing after all. However, the council were interested. They worked out a plan for publicising the local product. All farmers complain, of course, it's their nature, but down here they have something to complain about. The wine we make is decent honest stuff. Unfortunately the French are drinking less and less of it as a daily beverage, and the price hasn't gone up in line with the rest of the items in the Retail Price Index. So ONE: we would show a council meeting, in which the problems of dealing with rural poverty would get eloquent discussion. TWO: as I wanted to make the point that things are easier for the citizen in a French village than in a British one, because the people who matter are always on the spot, I would arrange to be filmed going up to the Mayor as he did some pruning in among the vines. I would ask him about my rates and then turn the conversation towards vine-pruning, and he would tell me how the older varieties of grape-vines, which used to produce vast quantities of rather poor stuff, were now being replaced by much nobler and nicer varieties. THREE: we would hold a village gathering – a sort of wine and cheese party – in the village hall, where all the local wines would be in prominent view on the table with their labels clearly visible; and various other little stunts, aimed at doing the village and the district some good, as well as doing even more good to the viewers throughout France. For did not Pasteur say that wine is the healthiest and most hygienic of all drinks?

So the TV people came down. It must have made a nice break for them. They hired a car at the airport and spent three days, staying at a good hotel ten miles away. Angélique, the producer, was a Parisienne of great charm, effortlessly capable of winding the most intractable member of the public round her little finger. She brought a cameraman and a sound engineer, who held the tape-recorder, and a lighting engineer, who hung around doing nothing. And how the rest of us worked, for a day and a half! I really think that if Angélique had asked us all to jump in the river stark naked or in our Sunday best, we'd have done it – and then done a re-take. Well, we did all the things the council had planned to do, and a few more. They got me up the tower winding the clock – I told you about that earlier. And they got the Mayor to pretend to conduct a wedding – in France all marriages have to be performed at the Mairie, and if you want a religious wedding you can go to the church afterwards. Wearing his mayoral sash, he made a speech to an imaginary couple saying how nice it was to be marrying two young people who were devoting their working lives to making delicious pure wine, the healthiest and most hygienic of all drinks. . . .

Yes, the film did get shown a few weeks later. All three minutes of it. There was me winding the clock, because it's very picturesque. And there was me going up to the Mayor in the vineyard, saying *Bonjour Monsieur Delmas* – but that's as far as that conversation got. It was followed by views of the village and its most picturesque inhabit-ants, with a voice-over by me with my picturesque accent saying how convenient it is to be able to get hold of the

Mayor at any time, etc., etc. Then one heard a lot of the villagers and *their* picturesque accents, milling around when the travelling grocer came. The meeting of the town council came down to about twenty seconds of picturesque local faces, with the proceedings reduced to 'I declare this meeting open'. The wedding speech was cut, but there was a good half minute of the jollifications in the village hall, though alas none of the pretty labels on the bottles was visible. These shots were followed by someone in the studio explaining how municipal councillors are elected. Very educational. I learned, by the way, that foreigners aren't eligible however good they are at clock-winding.

Well, I was a bit disappointed. It seemed a tiny result after all that fuss and bother. But to my surprise – and, I must say, pleasure – everybody else in the village was absolutely delighted. They and the village had been on the telly! People got letters from distant friends, relations and chance acquaintances, confirming the wondrous fact. When I was writing my pieces for *Le Monde* I used to get a few readers' letters from Paris, Brussels, New Zealand and Atlanta, Georgia, and other places where that paper is read. But nobody in the village – and hardly anyone in the little town where we go to market on Wednesdays – reads *Le Monde*. However, when I went shopping in that town the next day, I was astonished. 'Ooh, Monsieur Areece, we saw you on the telly!' Now I know that I really exist and I live in a village that is on the map. Well, no, not really. But we *were* on the map for at least twenty-four hours.

MUTTON ETC.

Whenever I'm in London, chatting with my children and my friends over such staple local dishes as taramasalata, octopus-and-chips, Peking duck and Black Forest gâteau, I think of myself as a cosmopolitan or a citizen of the world. But down here, in this little village in the inexpensive end of the south of France, I'm the local Englishman. And that involves me in Anglo-French relations.

The village is too small to have any shops. Monsieur Rancoul the butcher comes twice a week from the nearest town, driving his elaborately equipped van. The other day my wife Sophie was hesitating between a pound of toughish chunks for a boeuf bourguignon and a couple of nice little escalopes when Rancoul started teasing me. 'Why not have a leg of lamb this weekend, Monsieur Areece? Look at this beauty! *Vous pourriez vous régaler!*'

He's a kind man actually, but he thinks that all work and no play makes Jack a dull butcher, and he's unhappy if he can't work up a brisk debate on almost anything from football to the iniquities of the local police, who have taken to lurking in the bushes with their radar speed-check thing instead of standing boldly in the open and giving you time to slow down. I say he's kind, but his leg of lamb suggestion was to tease me into reacting. He knows perfectly well that for Sophie and me the price of living down here, among the wild scented hills, with good local wine at two pounds fifty a gallon at the pump, and oysters at a pound the dozen, not to mention Gauloises at sixty pence for twenty – the price of all this is abstaining from caviar, lobsters and legs of expensively educated French lamb. Beef isn't dear in France, nor maize-fed chickens that go jogging in the open air, but lamb and mutton cost a bomb.

What Rancoul was really on about was the fact that I, as the Englishman, am plotting to ruin French shepherds by flooding the country with the British product. The animals that thrive in England's green and pleasantly damp land are foreign, and must be inferior – otherwise why are they cheaper? *Le Dumping* he calls it. After selling all this stuff abroad, what do the perfidious English eat? The tasteless fibres of antipodean specimens dumped by New Zealanders, that race of barbarous rugby players who were so unkind about the *Rainbow Warrior* affair.

Of course I fell into his trap. His audience had drifted over from Monsieur Planas's grocery van, which comes at the same time. How delicious, I said, is lamb from New Zealand's pollution-free pastures. Pollution-free, that is, when he – Monsieur Rancoul – via his Ministry of Defence, isn't letting off nuclear bombs in the vicinity. And how much more delicious is a real, tender, juicy English cutlet! Why should Monsieur Rancoul and his chauvinistic politicians try to deprive French housewives of the right to roast whatever leg they choose? What about liberty, equality and fraternity, eh?

'Well,' he said, 'it all started with with your Madame Thatcher, didn't it? I mean to say, it was like getting blood out of a stone, making her pay her subscription to the Common Market and obey the rules. Mind you,' he said, 'as a hard-working, independent tradesman I couldn't help admiring her. If only your Madame Thatcher had been a Frenchwoman she'd have had my vote.'

My Madame Thatcher! I was fifteen when Chamberlain came back from Munich and I switched from the *Boy's Own Paper* to the *New Statesman*. I don't think my Churchill was a real Tory. And it isn't my Mr Kinnock either. When I'm in London people go on about my Monsieur Mitterrand. It's a hard life.

I was starting to attack Rancoul on the subject of his heavily subsidised butter mountain when Sophie remembered that she had been a good little Dutch girl before we got married. 'I'll start taking you seriously,' she said, 'when you obey the EEC directives and stop pouring your chemicals in the Rhine from your nasty potash mines in Alsace and poisoning the market gardens in Holland down at the other end. Shame on you!'

Rancoul looked quite capable of defending his right to chuck his waste products around as he pleases in Alsace – which, as it happens, is about 450 miles from here as the crow flies. But he wasn't going to be distracted. He kept his eyes firmly on me as he thumped the counter with a calf's foot. Madame Combadazou, Madame Delmas and little old Madame Roques pressed closer. Rancoul is a good performer, if a bit of a ham, and they enjoy him.

'Ah,' he said, 'you English! Perfidious Albion! You burnt Joan of Arc, didn't you?' Ho. Hum. I didn't think it would be much good explaining that in England Joan is a heroine. She comes into the same category as Dreyfus on Devil's Island. Queen Victoria, no left-winger, wrote to her Prime Minister: 'I am too horrified for words at this monstrous sentence against the poor martyr Dreyfus', and the average British schoolchild feels – or felt when I was at school – the same way or more so about Joan, who was done to death by the sort of untrustworthy foreigner who launched the Spanish Armada, paid Guy Fawkes, organised the St Bartholomew's Day massacre and (getting a bit muddled here) guillotined all those charming aristocrats. What a pity our Scarlet Pimpernel couldn't have saved Joan! Not much good, that line of argument, because one can hardly deny that Joan wasn't exactly fond of us at that time and place. However, I did point out that it was the Burgundians who sold Joan down the river and Burgundians are his lot not mine. And Cauchon, who sentenced her, was a very French bishop and the boss of the University of Paris as well – and if Rancoul didn't believe me I could go indoors and fetch my Petit Larousse to prove it.

At that point Rancoul burst out laughing. Common sense had broken through. 'All right,' he said. 'I agree. You didn't burn Joan of Arc. But you must admit it wasn't me, either.'

We shook hands on it. When it comes to burning people at the stake, we're against it. We're on the same side.

Still, it wasn't so long ago that Rancoul's peasant compatriots burnt a lot of British sheep and were very rude to

the lorry-drivers who were transporting them. The popular British press, the sort that has page three nudes and
very short paragraphs, took note and waxed indignant,
saying 'Yah boo, smelly Frogs!' and ruder words to that
effect. My neighbours knew all about that, because the
television showed them the offending front page. They
were rather shocked and puzzled. Was there some sinister
motive? they asked me. Was the dreaded Intelligence
Service behind it, or what? Why make such a fuss about a
fairly routine *manifestation*?

I tried to explain that *manifestations* are not part of the
normal British scene. We do have monster strikes every
five years or so, lasting weeks or months, with pitched
battles that get on international television. Years ago my
neighbours had seen and heard the Wapping business,
that year-long war between fine old Victorian printing
customs and word-processors and post-war machinery.
But they didn't realise that we don't go in much for manifesting. Manifesting is a French speciality, and they're
used to it. It's a short operation lasting an afternoon, or
sometimes a day, causing the maximum interference to
everyone while it lasts. It often involves building a barri-
cade or setting things on fire. It's accepted with tolerant
resignation like an Act of God. It isn't a strike. When there
are strikes they musn't go on too long or the people who
are grievously affected by them – people who need their
mail, for example, if it's a post office strike, or commuters,
if it's the Paris underground system – are liable after a
week or two to start manifesting themselves, against the
strikers, and that hurts the strikers' feelings.

Lorry-drivers frequently go in for fine manifestations,

causing monster traffic jams. Sometimes squads of them do this by driving extremely slowly on all lanes of a motorway (*opération escargot*, they call that) or blocking a frontier, to protest against all the many things that can get on a lorry driver's nerves, or indeed anybody else's.

But lorry-drivers are often on the receiving end. My immediate wine-making neighbours tend to stop Spanish wine-tankers and let the contents glug into the ditch. They occasionally chop down plane trees to block a road for an hour or two. And they have mass meetings, when they march around Montpellier or Narbonne for an afternoon, chanting anti-Brussels slogans and burning a tax office. The police prefer to stand around benevolently, letting a good manifestation be had by all, with nobody getting hurt. Arresting a manifester would be counterproductive and lead to a much more vigorous manifestation later. It is said that they take precautions to be sure that they are out-numbered.

Not long ago a chap I know was driving a lorry-load of melons from Spain when the local fruit-and-veg growers were having a manifestation. He was stopped by a posse. Two of them got into his lorry and accompanied him to a lay-by where the cargo could be conveniently destroyed. But there were two policemen there. My friend thought his wicked melons would get through safely. But the policemen said to the two manifesters: 'Look, there are two of us and one of him, so you're outnumbered. It won't do. We don't want a breach of the peace. If you can't get any reinforcements you'll have to let him go.' So the fruit-growers got busy on their walkie-talkie and six of their pals turned up in an overladen Renault 4. That made a quorum, so that the gendarmes could stand around philo-sophically while the melon-squashing took place. All very civilised, and after their afternoon's manifestation-therapy the fruit-and-veg growers felt much better. It alleviates occupational aches and pains, and there's always the hope that Paris and Brussels will take note.

One day last November Madame Roques' grandson Philippe went up to Paris to take part in the manifestation of the *lycéens*. *Lycéens* are roughly equivalent to grammar school and sixth-form college pupils, and they wanted better buildings, smaller classes and more supervisors to keep order in the playgrounds and corridors (which isn't part of a teacher's job in France). It was a great success. French Railways gave them cut-price tickets in the inter-ests of goodwill. A hundred thousand of them paralysed Paris for an afternoon. There was a certain amount of looting and sacking, mainly by young people who weren't *lycéens* at all. The government promised more money. Nobody was killed. Only a couple of dozen were injured, and they were policemen so (from some people's point of view) they didn't count. And everyone was peacefully back at school next day.

Giles Romilly and Michael Alexander wrote a book called *The Privileged Nightmare* about their life in the famous prisoner of war camp at Colditz. They say:

At times the tension was so powerful that it seemed as if it must crack the walls of the castle . . . The French regarded it as dangerous and sought deliberately to dis-perse it . . . If any man in their group was seen to be unhappy and brooding they did not, as the British way tended to be, leave him alone but pestered him until he admitted what was wrong . . . Often at night in the French quarters, when all was silent and dark, a prisoner would start to howl. Another prisoner would take up the howl, then another, till the night shrieked. After these outbursts, the French said, they felt better.

It seems to me that a manifestation is a sort of howl. Of course a howl is not a rational procedure, nor is it meant to be. One should not be taken in by the noises the French make about their alleged respect for logic, clear analysis, Cartesianism and all that, which applies only to the one per cent of the population that knows how to cope with their irritating written grammar, like the strange affair of the agreement of the past participle. France generally, *la France profonde*, loves its astrologers, acupuncturists, homeopathists, graphologists, and specialists in *désenvoûtement*. The last-named are handy whenever one has got bewitched – *envoûté* – and they advertise lavishly in the local papers. Getting bewitched is a fairly common misfortune. One's rabbits die, twinges are felt in the joints, or the tax man wants to have a look at the books. An able *désenvoûteur* can deal with the matter at a distance, if you phone her or him with the details and send a cheque by post. This saves travelling expenses.

Howling and manifesting may seem mad to us, when it affects us, but then our popular press seems a bit mad to them. Anyway, the average French person looks reasonably happy. As the popular British press knows and frequently proclaims, the French use less soap per head, or per foot, than the British. But on average they live sixteen months longer. Public howling may be better than private soaping.

I don't really believe in national character, not as far as individuals are concerned. But there's something in it when it comes to groups, and to what people know about the past. A little history is still on the syllabus in French schools, with the manifestations, barricades and upheavals from the Fall of the Bastille through 1830 and 1848 to 1958 and 1968, most of which are classified as Good Things. If you're in France and get delayed, or worse, by a manifestation, think of it as group psychotherapy. Or, of course, set up a howl yourself.

GARDENING MADE EASY

Once upon a time Sophie and I lived in Cornwall, just across the bridge from England. The winters are gentle there, thanks to the Gulf Stream. In fact the winters are very like the summers – soft wet west winds – except that in winter the days are shorter. One of our neighbours had a banana tree in his garden. Of course, he never got any bananas from it; you mustn't ask too much of the Gulf Stream. We had a fig tree, and every two or three years it produced a pound of figs.

I love catalogues: mail order catalogues, firework catalogues and especially seedsmen's lists. They used to fire me with horticultural ambitions. Frankly, I'm a rotten gardener. 'Slapdash, impulsive, given to rushing his fences and sadly lacking in long-term application' – that was what my most perceptive school report said. It made an accurate change from 'Could do better if he tried'. What I like growing are things that pop up quickly and do something interesting, like producing giant pumpkins, or trapping insects in their flowers and eating them, or shooting seeds all over the place.

Years ago in Cornwall I saw something in a specialist

seed catalogue that I simply had to have. It sounded sensational: hairy, poisonous, a bit of a climber, a distant cousin of the melon family. It was advertised as producing fuzzy fruits which, when ripe, would explode at the slightest touch, like a finely tuned mousetrap, and project a shrapnel shower of small hard seeds in a jet of sticky liquid. *Ecballium elaterium*, it was called, or the squirting cucumber. Irresistible.

So I bought the precious packet. And for three years I tried everything: plant pots on the radiator; sowing at the new moon; nourishing feeds of animal, vegetable and mineral origin; magnetism; distilled water; holy water; water from Dozmary Pool where King Arthur threw Excalibur . . . No joy at all. Perhaps it was that temperate climate, which really does push temperance to excess. I gave it up.

And then we moved down here, in the unfashionable part of the south of France. One August evening in our first year Sophie and I went for a walk. On the scrubby strip of ground between the roadway and the vineyards we admired the exotic weeds – Jerusalem sage, blue thistles, stinking everlasting (it smells of curry), lizard orchids, soft storksbill, Maltese cross – with exotic beasties on them: green shield beetles, praying mantises, the *ephippigère de Béziers* that looks as though it's got an enormous sting (but it's only its egg-laying tube) and little grasshoppers with blue or red wings. And suddenly Sophie said: 'Look at that funny hairy thing like a miniature melon plant! It's got little baby melons on it . . .'

She bent down to pick one. And was absolutely galvanised. 'Oh!' she said, 'it went off like a bomb! Those seeds are hard; they hurt. And I've got sticky stuff on my hands. What a horrid plant! It gave me quite a turn.'

It was delighful. I'd got my *ecballium elaterium* without lifting my little finger. In the local patois it's *cocobre d'ase*, or donkey's cucumber. There are a lot of them around, hiding here and there. Nowadays Sophie and I keep an eye on the state of ripeness of their little fruits, so that innocent visitors from England can have a stimulating surprise. Prehistoric humour, satisfaction guaranteed, and no digging needed.

In our second year Monsieur Combadazou wanted to sell us a vineyard. It's hidden between the cemetery and the garrigue. The garrigue is what they call the wild moorland where the sheep graze in the winter and the spring, until they are taken fifty miles away by lorry, to hills where the grass stays green in summer. We knew this vineyard already, because it's where we go to pick kitchen herbs such as rosemary and thyme among the dead vine stumps. It's in a narrow valley out of the north wind. There are cypress trees around, and nightingales and hoopoes and bee-eaters. Monsieur Combadazou also has twenty acres of vineyard on the plain which he deals with by tractor, but you can't get a tractor into this hidden vineyard. The only way in is along a narrow path with a rock face on one side and a ten-foot drop to a stream bed – dry except after a heavy rainstorm – on the other. Before the war they used donkey-power and manpower, but that sort of slow work doesn't pay nowadays. So the vineyard was left to itself, and had gone wild.

Monsieur Combadazou thought that as I hadn't got anything much to do (writing isn't thought of as work, of course, except by writers, and there's a lot of time spent sitting in the sun or the shade with an exercise book and a cooling drink, lost in thought) – not having much to do, as I said – I might pass the time by grubbing everything up by hand and planting superior varieties of vine, little by little. Good, healthy open-air exercise, that. After all, everybody ought to have a vineyard: he would kindly let me have it for a mere franc, or ten pence, per square metre. It's a hectare, two and a half acres, 10000 square metres. A thousand pounds. Given away, or almost. And he hinted that he might be open to offer.

What a temptation! We would be like Adam and Eve. What would we do with this secret paradise? No new vines: that we agreed on straight away. There's more than enough wine produced round here, and when you're surrounded by professionals who are happy to sell you a gallon of harmless necessary plonk for the price of a couple of pints of beer in England, it seems a pity to deprive them of that pleasure. To say nothing of the sweat of the brow.

What we thought we might do was create a Mediterranean garden. Nothing outlandish; no banana trees or ornamental peanuts, just a few handsome species that would look right under that sky, as blue as a Gauloise packet 300 days a year. An arbutus, some clumps of pistachio terebinth for their shining berries and turpentiny smell, a bay tree and some herbs to go round it, an Aleppo pine, some prickly juniper, a few olive trees, a Judas tree for its pink flowers on naked branches in spring, and of course some almonds for blossom in February and nuts later, and what about a *micocoulier*, sometimes translated

as a nettle-tree? It doesn't sting and it provides all-wood
pitchforks if you train the branches when they're young.

We went round that long narrow hectare, consulting
our naturalist's handbook as we wandered. Yes, we'd put
a cypress here and an arbutus there. But look! Near that
rock there's a fine arbutus. And over there, how elegant
those cypresses look! And those almonds round the edge
would have won full marks from Capability Brown.
Really, the garden had got it right all by itself. Judas tree
and *micocoulier* and all. No need to make any changes. Just
a little tinkering in winter and spring. Pre-war vineyard
owners had always planted the odd cherry tree and
almond tree here and there, with a rose bush at the end of
every other row of vines. They don't do that any more,
now that machinery has taken over from donkeys and
horses and villagers with very low cash incomes. As I've
explained, this isn't an area that produces precious vin-
tages with a bouquet that wine writers go on about – just
plain ordinary red wine, to be sold almost as soon as it's
made. There's a lot of it, too much in fact, and to make a
living from that sort of wine you have to cut out the frills
and think about efficiency and productivity and market-
ing. No rose bushes or cherry trees. Well, we could plant a
few new ones when the spirit moved us.

But we would have to protect our purchase. If you own
a garden you don't want outsiders coming galumphing
in, laughing and yelling, playing hide-and-seek and picnicking to the sound of ghetto-blasters. Perhaps a ten-
foot-high stone wall, with bits of broken bottles cemented
on the top? That would cost a bomb, and we were short of
bombs. We would have only just enough money to buy

the garden if we beat Combadazou down to something near half price. What about barbed wire? But then there are rabbits and hares and pheasants and even the occasional wild boar. That means locals with shot-guns, who might have pliers in their pockets. Perhaps we would need a watch-tower and a shot-gun ourselves.

We gathered a few bay leaves from the old tree on the edge of the dried-up stream bed, and sat down to do a serious cost-benefit analysis. And we realised that, apart from Madame Mazel and Madame Delmas, who come once in a blue moon to gather herbs, and our friend Ernest Gal who does a little stalking at dawn in the shooting season, we were the only people who ever came there. To find this garden you have to know where it is. And to enjoy it in total tranquillity you don't need anything more.

So we didn't buy it. And we've still got it. Like the *ecballium elaterium*. You'll be welcome to both if you come down here.

I don't want you to think that I'm lazy. Dear me no. Life is real, life is earnest, and I do have to do some active gardening, or rather vegetable-growing. Although the locals grow flowers, they grow them in pots and tubs – geraniums and suchlike – for balconies and terraces and outside the front door. When they talk about a garden, a *jardin* (or *jardang* down here), they mean an allotment with a water supply, and they very kindly fixed me up with one soon after we settled here. They think every able-bodied male ought to have his own tomatoes, and it would have been rude to refuse. You grow tomatoes up seven-foot-high bamboo structures like small Eiffel Towers joined together, and they have to be strong enough to resist our north wind, which is a cousin of the mistral and the tramontane. If your first tomato isn't ripe by the Fourteenth of July they make sympathetic remarks to your wife and give her a kilo or two of theirs. Very humiliating. After that, it's tomatoes with everything. In England you have a green tomato problem, but we have a red tomato one. The housewives try to cope with it by making their own tomato concentrate, boiling down kilos of the things, straining out the skins and pips and boiling down again. It would be simpler, and vastly cheaper in terms of man hours and housewife hours, and probably in money terms too, to buy the stuff in cans or tubes. But that's what gardening does for you. It's a perverse activity leading to pride, envy, anger, back-ache and too many tomatoes.

Where we live it's bone-dry for most of the summer, and our veggies are where they are because of the unlimited spring water. So twice a week there's the watering chore, making and breaking little muddy dams to flood the channels between the rows of plants. I do that soon after dawn, not that I like getting up early but because it's far too hot later on. It gives me an excuse for a nice long siesta between French lunch time and British tea time. Of course when one has visitors from Tooting or Aberdeen it's gratifying to show off one's melons, aubergines, sweet peppers and giant pumpkins all basking out there in the open, but please don't be too jealous. You lucky people have such nice soft regular rain doing the watering for you, and bringing out those nourishing ecological snails.

When we do have a shower out come the snails and out

come the gardeners, rejoicing that they won't have to do any watering today or tomorrow and swinging their catch in plastic carrier-bags. A squishy business, that, and the game keeps on climbing out of the bag. After that you have to starve them for three weeks in case they've been eating any plants that are good for snails but bad for people. Madame Mazel keeps hers in an old bird cage in her cellar. We don't go in for snailing, ourselves, though we have them sometimes in a restaurant. The best thing about them is the parsley-garlic-and-butter filling, and the ritual with the snail-dish, snail-tongs and snail-fork. They aren't cheap. You can see tins of them in the posher supermarkets, imported from Eastern Europe, with little boxes of shells to go with them, or deep-frozen and ready-stuffed in the deep-freeze, costing about six pounds the pound. It's a tribute to the French talent for turning what was once food for the starving peasantry before the Revolution into something for conspicuous consumption on the expense account. It's the same thing with frogs' legs, which come deep-frozen from Indonesia.

Yes, well, you fortunate islanders have got nice rain and fat snails, and I hope you're duly grateful. What's more, you haven't got Colorado beetles. We have – big battalions of them. They look like giant ladybirds, about half an inch long, with stripes instead of spots. If you see a pair on your potato plants on Monday and don't pick them off, by Saturday they and their larvae will have eaten every leaf. Even the French haven't found a way to turn them into an acceptable supper dish. Their French name is *doryphores*, and that's also what they called the occupying German troops during the war, because they were supposed to live on a diet of potatoes too. And that reminds me: several times I've been told that Colorado beetles came to Europe when the American Air Force dropped them on the German potato fields in the war in the hope of depriving the Nazis of their staple nourishment. Quite untrue, of course. Colorado beetles were chomping their way everywhere on this side of the Channel long before the war. But it's one of those persistent popular myths, like the one about the War Office secretly lacing NAAFI tea with bromide to reduce the libido of the British forces. Somebody ought to gather up all these myths some time.

When the Colorado beetles have increased and multiplied on the potatoes they move on to the aubergines. So there's another twice-weekly chore – beetle picking. Gardeners keep a beady eye on one another's *jardins*, and if I were to let my lettuces get too thirsty or my Colorado beetles too well-fed, my name would be mud.

Really, it would be a luxury to go out and buy just as many tomatoes and leeks and sweet peppers as we want, and have more time to idle in Monsieur Combadazou's abandoned vineyard, listening to the nightingales and admiring the busy multicoloured insects. But that's life, I suppose. One has to keep up appearances.

SCHOOL

There's been a great kerfuffle in our village. We nearly lost our school. It started because of the amorous activities of a travelling fairground man who runs the dodgem cars. The French call them *autos tamponneuses*, by the way, which doesn't imply dodging but bumping. That's a more accurate description of the kind of fun the younger locals like when the fair comes at midsummer and around Christmas to the market town, four miles away.

Well, this dodgem operator. Anaïs Vidal ran away with him. Before I say anything more, I must apologise. Editors of respectable newspapers and magazines, and even the BBC occasionally, allow all kinds of four-letter words these days, but any reference to adult female persons as 'girls' is out. It's sexist. Similarly, 'blondes' and 'brunettes', and even more so 'smashing blondes' and 'luscious brunettes' are taboo: they're patronising labels used by macho males. OK, and I'm all for the dignity of the human being, whether female, male or uncertain. But Anaïs had, and no doubt still has, an old-fashioned mentality. I'm sure she would hate to be called a fair-haired female. If I call her a smashing blonde it's because I'm certain that that's what she'd like me to call her. She looked rather like Gina Lollobrigida in those dear old post-war Italian films, though Gina was a dark-haired person. As a matter of fact Anaïs was what we call a Mediterranean blonde, and they are blackish at the roots if you get close enough to see. Persons who dye their hair like that, in this old-fashioned part of the world, seem to do so in the hope of influencing other persons in an old-fashioned sort of way.

So Anaïs slipped away in the small hours one morning, leaving a note on the breakfast table. As soon as he read it, her husband François dashed off to the market town to block their joint account, getting there just in time. We couldn't understand why Anaïs had left him. François is a kindly chap with twenty acres of productive vineyards, and looks like a slim young Marlon Brando. The villagers who had seen the dodgem man reported that he was a short hairy fellow with gold teeth, quite unprepossessing compared with our François, and why anyone should prefer the hairy man and his caravan and dodgem track was more than the old ladies on the bench in the village square could understand, though they spent several afternoons advancing theories about it. We don't eavesdrop, of course, but the favourite places for sitting and knitting in the village square are not far from our kitchen window, and the discussions that happen to drift our way are so good for our language studies.

Cyrille, aged seven, Serge, aged six and Michel, aged four, didn't seem to turn a hair when their mother disappeared. François' house and his mother and father's house are really two parts of the same building. The older village houses are like that: they form a sort of long irregular terrace, easily subdivided by bricking up a connecting doorway, and just as easily re-combined if it seems convenient to do so. François' mother and her unmarried sister Mademoiselle Estelle, who lives on the other side, seemed to cope with the three children effectively and philosophically, making remarks like 'I told you so' to their friends. Anaïs hasn't been seen again, but it's reported that she operates a very pretty merry-go-round next to the dodgems as the travelling fun fair circulates around the Midi. The thing seemed to have settled down to a nine days' wonder.

And what, you ask, has all this got to do with our village school? Patience. First you must have the data. Our primary school is one of the best in Europe, or in the world. That's not just because of Madame Martin, though she's a very good *institutrice* or teacher. She's a vigorous *femme forte*, which is polite French for a stout party. She doesn't encourage a lot of creativity or self-expression, but she has a passionate belief in the three Rs, and gets them over by force of personality. But the school's trump card at the time I'm talking about was that it had eight pupils.

Perhaps eight is the right number for a primary school with a vigorous adaptable teacher. And Madame Martin *is* adaptable. One winter a Scottish university lecturer rented a house in the village, with his wife and a pair of nine-year-old twins. He'd been given sabbatical leave and was writing a book. The law and Madame Martin allowed him to send the twins to the school, and it worked out to everyone's satisfaction, even the twins',

85

because Madame Martin seized the opportunity. The three Rs went on as usual, but the village children learnt some English, or rather Scottish, and at the end of term the twins were prattling away happily in French, with a beautiful Midi accent. The news even got round the village that Scotland isn't in England, a fact that very few French people know.

I learnt something myself, thanks to the Franco-Scottish project that Madame Martin got up. In the fifteenth century, when Scotland was an independent country, Scots mercenaries were fighting on the French side in the Hundred Years' War. The Stuart family was prominent among these warriors, and Charles VII of France gave John Stuart the town of Aubigny-sur-Nère as a reward. That was in Joan of Arc's time. The Stuarts prospered there, and built themselves a nice château. They died out when Charles II was on our throne, and Louis XIV took back the property. King Charles had a French female friend, Louise de Kéroualle. She did even better out of the liaison than Charles's other female friends. It was Louise who got Nell Gwyn into the books of quotations. Louise was unpopular, because she was not only expensive but also fairly well known to be a French agent. The London mob was about to throw stones at Nell Gwyn's carriage, because they had mistaken it for Louise's, when Nell stood up and shouted: 'Be civil, good people! I am the *Protestant* whore!' – and got a round of applause. Charles made Louise the Duchess of Portsmouth, and their son was made Duke of Richmond. When Charles died, Louise went back to France, and was given a present by Louis XIV: Aubigny-sur-Nère and the château. The other day I went to see it. Louise gave the town a park, which is still called Le Jardin de la Duchesse de Portsmouth. She ended her life as a pious benevolent old lady. There's a family tree in the château, from which I learnt that one of the descendants of the Duke of Richmond is our present Princess of Wales. It's a small world.

Another thing is that Madame Martin lives on the spot. Her husband – but of course – grows grapes for a living. That's what the village is for. They live in a flat, above the schoolroom. She knows her pupils many a month before they're born. Of course when they're eleven, off they go by bus to the big school in town, as is right and proper at that age. But until then they're in their own village, everybody keeps an eye on them, and Madame Martin is always there for a chat with parents, grandparents, aunts and uncles about the latest directives from the Ministry of Education, or Grandma's rheumatism, or what was on last night's TV or why little Georges needs to learn the multiplication table even though he's got a pocket calculator. It's a climate of mutual confidence.

And it does make a difference. The village knows all about it, ever since the dreaded Children of the North, *les enfants du Nord*, came as tenants of a holiday villa for the whole of one August. There seemed to be a dozen of them. In the course of their nocturnal debauches they screeched, machine-gunned (tagadagada is what you yell if you're a small French child) and changed gear race-track style (brrrm, brrrm, brrrm) until the small hours, stamping round the little streets and in and out of the square – and one does like to have one's windows open on August nights. Then they seemed to sleep it off until midday, before getting on once more with pillaging (they had an unsuccessful go at the phone box), assault-and-battery (they kicked the Mayor's shins when he tried to stop them stoning his chickens), fire-raising (they set a rubbish bin alight, but luckily it was noticed, thus preventing the pine wood going up in flames) and generally creating alarm and despondency and being discourteous to Senior Citizens. One day someone managed to count them. There were in fact only four of them in all, ranging in age from five to nine. Their mother was a pale weary figure, rarely seen. She found the strength to explain apologetically one day to Madame Mazel that they normally lived shut up in a tower block in an industrial town near the Belgian border, and that on holiday in the village they were *déchaînés*. Literally that means 'unchained', but it has strong implications of all hell being let loose. Their father, reasonably enough, preferred to spend his holiday at home, allegedly putting up shelves and doing some useful paintwork. The villagers have a lot of patience with children off-duty, but there were mutterings of 'Chain 'em up again'. The village under-elevens aren't angels but, largely thanks to Madame Martin and the way the school interacts with the population, they seem to be on the way to becoming reasonable human beings as well as readers, writers and adder-uppers.

Next year that villa was rented by Nicolette, a charming young widow from Toulouse, with her two nice civilised young children, one of each. That was six months after Anaïs had disappeared. As you can guess, one thing led to another, and before we knew what was happening François and Nicolette announced that as soon as François' divorce came through they were going to get married. It seemed a jolly good idea from all points of view. Of course one doesn't get married to please one's friends and relations, but if everybody looks happy about it and says how sensible and lucky one is it adds to the euphoria.

Alas, doom was impending. Nicolette had a nice house in a suburb of Toulouse. And François, who has a qualification from an agricultural college, was offered a job there. All very satisfactory, you might think.

But three from eight leaves five. If François and Nicolette and her two children *and* Cyrille, Serge and Michel went to live happily ever after in Toulouse, then Cyrille, Serge and Michel would cease to be on the school roll. The word soon went round that a bureaucrat in an office somewhere had said: 'Eight pupils are OK, just, but if you have only five I'll have to kill off your school. And if that deals a fatal wound to your village, too bad. Sorry.'

That would mean the school bus. And unknown teachers. And school dinners, with the children home just to sleep and for days off and holidays. They'd be foreigners. They wouldn't belong to the village any more, and the village wouldn't belong to them.

Not only that. There would be no going back. We learnt about the regulations. A one-teacher school with eight pupils can be allowed to exist if it's there already. But once it's been closed you've reached a point of no return. If we lost François' three and the school closed, and then next year Mother Hubbard and Father Hubbard and ten children moved into the village, it would be no good saying: 'We had five pupils and you closed us; now we've

got fifteen – can we please start up again?' To open a school you need at least twenty pupils, and in fact the authorities prefer something like forty. One-teacher schools are thought to be out of date and inefficient. No doubt there's something in the official point of view. Our Madame Martin suited the village, but if you had a run-of-the-mill teacher living somewhere else who just came in by car to give the lessons and then went off again, looking forward to promotion to a bigger and better school, it wouldn't be the same. Legislators can't make exceptions for particular situations or for Madame Martin.

That kind of crisis has hit many a village, especially in areas where the countryside has become de-populated. There are picturesque villages up in the hills that look very fine and happy at Easter and in the summer because that is when the people from Paris and Hampstead and elsewhere are having a good time in the holiday houses that they bought from villagers who've sold up and gone to live in town. But those villages have lost their school. If you look at French papers that go in for classified advertisements of houses and flats to let, you'll see some absolute bargains – reserved for tenants with several children of primary school age. Now you know why. The houses belong to village councils, and the village wants to keep its school.

So we had a month of gloom and suspense. Nicolette and her children stayed on for a while, and everyone was very nice to them. They helped François with his vintage, which is a good test of character because it's hard work out there in the sun, filling plastic buckets with grapes. And – to cut what must have been a long story short – we learnt one day that Nicolette had fallen in love with the village as well as with François. She wanted to stay. Now she's a full-time vineyard owner's wife. She sold her house in Toulouse, which paid for an extra ten acres of vineyard that happened to be on sale, and a new tractor-sprayer . . . And of course instead of eight children on the roll, Madame Martin now has ten.

And there was a very happy wedding. The village is proud of François. He did a splendid job.

THE TELEPHONE

*F*rance has got a splendid telephone system. It's even better than the British one. Don't close the book in patriotic indignation, please. I cannot tell a lie. And anyway, Radio Four is much better than anything the French have on offer. (The fish and chips at Broadcasting House are super.)

But once upon a time the French phone was the despair of businessmen and journalists. That was because of General de Gaulle, some people say. He was a brilliant writer, and he loved the written French language. People ought to write well-expressed letters, he thought, not mumble into telephones. A neat pile of letters in the morning is better than bells jangling at odd moments. In his day you had to wait years to get a phone, and from ordinary phone boxes you could only make local calls. If you were travelling in France and wanted to phone England you had to go to a post office and undertake tedious negotiations.

In our village in the early 1970s there was no post office. Unless you were one of the half-dozen lucky people with a phone at home, you had to go and knock at

Monsieur Rataboul's door. He had the official public phone, and if he or Madame Rataboul were in, they worked the apparatus for you. You sat in their little parlour among the family photographs. After your conversation the operator would ring the Ratabouls and tell them what to charge. I suppose this left them a small margin to compensate for the nuisance. Anyway, they seemed to enjoy being at this nerve-centre of village life. Almost every day someone would phone, usually for the doctor, and then there would be time for a chat afterwards. They were retired, and *'Ça passe le temps'* – it passes the time – as Madame Rataboul told me.

Then in 1976 Monsieur Rataboul died, and Madame Rataboul moved to her married daughter's place in Perpignan, a long way away. By this time things were looking up, telephonically. They put up a proper phone box in the village square. It was a smart one, made of aluminium, glass and yellow plastic. It's true that it didn't really go with the square. With its golden stone, grey and ochre stucco, Roman-style tiles, roses round the doors and the mulberry tree in the middle, our square had looked like an opera set. You almost expected sopranos and contraltos to enter, left, as a chorus of peasant girls tripping from the church, while a posse of gendarmes – tenors and basses – marched in from behind the pump on the right, ringing up the curtain with a rousing commercial about our local Languedoc wine before getting down to the serious business of love and murder with Joan Sutherland and Placido Thingummy. The high-tech phone box brought the whole thing down to earth.

But we were glad to have it. Alas, the apparatus inside

had its peculiarities. It had four modes of operation.

In mode number one, everything was free. That mode never lasted long, but the news spread rapidly on the grape-vine. Our friend Alison has parents in Boston, Massachusetts, and garrulous friends in San Francisco, so she would zoom over on her moped from her village, ten miles away, where the phone box was made of sterner stuff. She's doing well now, selling her paintings in London, Zurich and New York, but in those days, fifteen years ago, she used to chew her way through sacks of economical brown rice from the Camargue. Look after the centimes and the francs will look after themselves, she used to say.

In mode number two it worked in the conventional manner: that was for about three-quarters of the time. Madame Mazel, Madame Julie and the others sitting on the bench in the shade of the mulberry tree listened in politely, and you fed the thing with coins whenever it bleeped at you.

In mode number three it rang at the other end in the normal way, but the slots at our end refused to accept any money at all. You could hear the person you were trying to phone saying *'Allo, allo'* and other remarks in increasing irritation until he or she rang off. Very frustrating.

In mode number four the machine took in our coins and kept them, but gave absolutely nothing in return. From the point of view of the person one was trying to phone, it was just the same as mode number three, but at our end it led to cries of *'merde'* or worse, scattering the swallows under the eaves and silencing the cicadas.

After I'd been had two or three times by mode four I

wrote a polite complaint to the Big Telephone Chief at Montpellier. He replied with even greater courtesy, saying that all one has to do is go to the nearest post office and tell one's story – armed, of course, with an identity card, or a passport in my case, because in France they never believe you are who you say you are even when it doesn't matter two hoots. And then the kind post office person will give you your money back. Very nice of them. But still . . .

The Mayor drew up a petition. It was signed by all those who had tried to collaborate with the machine or who had resisted it with thumps and kicks – and by Fulcrand Combadazou, who said he knew where he could get some dynamite. And two months later, to our friend Alison's disappointment, we got a factory-fresh apparatus which worked impeccably. And, some years after that, they changed it for an even better model with liquid crystal display on a little screen. It even gives you change. Splendid!

Well, not quite splendid. The earlier model had a buzzer, and we knew its number. By then the waiting time for a phone had dropped from two years to a fortnight, but there were still people who refused to be wired up. Their friends could ring the box, preferably in fine weather, and the ladies sitting on the bench would do the rest. If they weren't there, you could rely on Pélagie Bezombes. Her terrace overlooks the square, and she's almost always on it. You might call her the village concierge or watchperson. She likes to know what goes on, and she's very useful. When we go out we usually tell her where we're going and when we'll be back. That keeps her happy, and if anyone comes to see us she can tell them how long they'll have to wait, or take a message – and if they won't talk she gives us a full and frank description of them. If the phone box buzzed when no one was in the square, she would only too willingly dash down, pick up the receiver and act as one's personal secretary. She has one of those piercing voices that would be useful in the Australian outback, and when she called '*Monsieur Areece! Le téléphone!*' I could hear her in the most intimate corner of our house.

But the new phone had no buzzer and no bell. I mentioned this to M. Cros the postman. He was shocked at what had been going on. 'What!' he said, 'people knew the number? It's meant to be a secret. And when they put the box in, they should have disconnected the buzzer – it's only there for technicians, when they install it or repair it. All your goings-on have been quite unauthorised. Tut tut.' I asked him why. He had no convincing explanation. Regulations are regulations.

That was in 1980, and at that time I was writing that series of would-be humorous articles for *Le Monde*. I mentioned the situation, and told the readers that in Britain the number is exhibited in each phone box, and people can ring you back when you've run out of coinage: so useful for long heart-to-heart conversations between lovers who have no phone at home or have good reason not to wish to use it when there's a third party around.

Now the French are brisk grumblers when it comes to grumbling about *la belle France*, but they can be touchy when criticism comes from barbarians bred in the outer darkness. A week later the editor wrote a piece about *la*

bataille des cabines téléphoniques. Apparently the paper had had a sackful of readers' letters, attacking – and sometimes defending – everything British, from Mrs Thatcher (who hadn't been Prime Minister long) downwards. He printed two of them.

One was from a Monsieur Lefèvre of Paris. He denounced what he called Britain's medieval telephone boxes, eternally re-painted in shocking red, and the cumbersome coins you had to keep feeding them with. After rambling on about this and that he ended with: 'No, I don't envy them their railways, or their roads, or their telephones, or their London Underground, or their food, or their economy, or their taxation. The only things I lift my hat to them for are the way they respect pedestrians on their zebras, and their nice clean public lavatories.'

I was glad to know that when Monsieur Lefèvre felt homesick in London he was able to cross the road to find somewhere quiet to be alone in. Since 1980 the public lavatory situation seems to have deteriorated in England. Whenever I'm in London I find that yet another gents has been abolished, or replaced by one of those horrid French-made *sanisettes*: one-holers, with a queue of impatient gentlemen hopping up and down outside, instead of those old-fashioned multiple facilities. As for zebras, he's quite right. A French zebra should be thought of as a suggestion of where you might consider taking your life in your hands, with your wits about you. They paint them lavishly. There are three in a 100-yard stretch of village road that I pass through every day, and I never think of stopping because there are hardly any inhabitants. British zebras are few and far between, and the driver knows that there will probably be someone on them. But that's a red herring. So, of course, are the old phone boxes with their many layers of red paint. How wrong Monsieur Lefèvre was! We did away with those splendid Victorian structures, and no sooner had we done so than they became highly desirable. Now you see second-hand ones all over the world. The other day I was in the very French town of Angers. There, lording it in a pedestrian square in the best part of town, was a dear old red British phone box, exiled and given a loving home. So sucks to Monsieur Lefèvre.

The other letter the editor printed was more to the point. It said: 'Why is it impossible to ring a public phone box? Because of reversed-charge calls! A wicked subscriber would ask for a reversed-charge call to a public box number. His accomplice, waiting there by arrangement, would accept the call . . . and when the phone people wanted to send the bill they would find, surprise, surprise, that they were trying to send it to a phone box; that is, to themselves. QED.'

I would like to flatter myself that I'd started something, but I don't think it was me. The wish to phone a phone box must have occurred to thousands of French people ever since telephones began. Anyway, two years later, in April 1982, the Minister of Posts, Telegraphs and Telephones was goaded into a reply in the Chamber of Deputies. He was reported as saying: 'There are a number of reasons why it is impossible to ring a phone box. People who live nearby would complain about the bell. You might have a crowd of people hanging around, all convinced that the next call would be for them. Someone might monopolise the box, just standing in it and waiting for a call. And of course there's the reversed-charge situation . . .' And he went on about that. Absolutely impossible, he said.

Another two and a half years went by. Despite the Minister, brains got to work, and at the end of 1984 a notice suddenly appeared in our phone box and in all the other ones in France: THIS CABIN CAN BE RUNG AT THE FOLLOWING NUMBER: . . . Bravo! The French say: *'Impossible n'est pas français'* – 'Impossible is not a French word'. Quite right. Just give them time.

Since then, French telephonic progress has known no limits: phonecards, and silicon chips with everything. Not only do you get three phones per house installed in no time, with buttons to press that squeak at different pitches instead of wheels that dodder around, but for a mere couple of pounds a month extra you can have a Minitel. It's a neat little computer terminal supplied by the phone people. Tap out the right code on the keyboard, and you get anyone's phone number in the whole of France, on the screen, almost instantly. Tap SNCF and your proposed points of departure and arrival, and the right bits of the railway timetable appear. Same thing for roads. Tap MICHELIN and whether you want scenery or speed or whatnot, and the clever thing flashes your itinerary on the screen. My bank has given me a secret code and if I feel I want my bank statement at three in the morning or any other time, any day, there it is, up to the minute, shining at me. Tap BBC, and there are the news headlines in English.

The latest models have a cunning and very necessary

dodge. You can invent a password for yourself, and the thing won't work unless you tap it out. That stops your children ruining you. Although it's free for directory enquiries, and ordinary services cost only about twenty centimes a minute, there are other services that cost more because the provider gets a cut. There are computer games that cost forty centimes a minute, for example, and intelligence tests. I scored a very low IQ on that, because I rushed my answers, and at 40 centimes a minute I bet you would too. There are hundreds of services you can tap into, frivolous or deadly serious. I got my Minitel only last month, and I look forward to hours of fun. I don't use a password because Sophie is the only other person in the house and she refuses to tangle with this new-fangled box. So there's no risk of what happened to some friends of ours. They went away for a weekend soon after their Minitel arrived and they left their children, aged eight to eighteen, at home. They spent a whole Sunday on the Minitel. Very educational, I'm sure, but the eventual phone bill caused alarm and despondency.

If the Minitel arrives in Britain one day, rejoice but beware. There's a special number you can tap out, which means: 'I've forgotten my password; please let me invent a new one'. If your children get hold of that, ruin stares you in the face. Keep the box under lock and key.

What a long way France has come, telephonically, since General de Gaulle retired. I'm told that a whirring noise can be heard at Colombey-les-Deux-Eglises. It's him, turning in his grave. Hardly anybody ever writes these days, despite the fact that the Ministry of Education has just made the spelling easier. But that's another story.

AROUND

*U*nless you go to Montpellier or are rash enough to try to pass through bottle-neck zones on the main through roads at peak weekends in the holiday season, you won't find any traffic jams round our way. The situation must be more clogged up in Great Britain, where the average member of the public who listened to my radio series on living in the Midi was a charming, intelligent person sitting in a motionless motor-car. I've actually received some fan letters. That shows what a lot of nice people are in a jam. All of them asked 'Where is this place you call your village? And is it all true, or are you making it up?'

Oh yes, it's true all right. I haven't got much imagination, and most of what I have was exhausted in changing my neighbours' names. They mustn't know that I've been making personal remarks about them to charming intelligent people in British traffic jams. I like all this fame and wealth, but I wouldn't want to hurt their feelings. For the same reason I won't tell you just where the village is. But here are a few clues.

It's certainly in the Midi. If one says 'the south of

France' it suggests millionaires and yachts, a lotus land of champagne, film stars and lobsters. In fact the Midi is the whole of the bottom third of France, a lot of it up on 3000-foot-high plateaux in the Massif Central, where it can be colder than the north of Scotland in winter, and where the sneezing shepherds carry big heavy-duty umbrellas most of the rest of the year.

You know you are in the Midi when the language changes. Up in Paris a big box of matches is *'Une grosse boîte d'allumettes'* – six syllables. In the Midi it s *'un*E *gross*E *boît*E *d'allumett*ES' – ten syllables. Bread and wine, *pain et vin*, become *pang et vang*.

It's bigger than England. Dotted all over it you come across various sorts of British subject. On the far right, by the sea, there's a narrow intensely crowded coastal strip, which we call the Riviera and the French call the Côte d'Azur. It was invented by the British in the last century. Queen Victoria loved it and streets are named after her, and nobody thought of being there in the summer because it's far too hot. Between the wars Somerset Maugham bought himself a mini-palace there. Lesser lights like Aldous Huxley, Scott Fitzgerald, and the Bloomsberries went down by the Blue Train, and people started to like being too hot – so the luxury hotels began to stay open in July and August. Nowadays it's even more crowded, you can hardly find room to lie down on the sand, and because there are no tides in the Mediterranean they have to send municipal employees out cleaning the beaches every morning in the posh resorts. The crime rate is higher than in Paris, and the average age of the British population is much lower than it used to be. As well as slow-moving retired gentlefolk there are whizz-kids in the high-tech industries that have started up on the strip, and sharp operators eagerly wheeling and dealing. As you may gather, people who live in the Midi but not on the Riviera suffer from a bad case of sour grapes.

Far over on the left of the Midi, near the Atlantic end of the Pyrenees, there's Pau. That was where characters in Anthony Trollope's novels used to have to go if they were *ruined*. In the 1850s a Scottish doctor set up shop there, claiming the climate was good for people with consumption or syphilis or both. What with them and the ruined – who built themselves modest twelve-bedroomed houses in a couple of acres of ground each, pigging it with just half a dozen servants – the British population expanded. It's not surprising that the first race track and golf course in France were at Pau. One must do something to pass the time. Field-Marshal Lord Alanbrooke's father was Master of the Pau Foxhounds 100 years ago. Today Pau is a nice place, with a splendid view of the mountains, but the French have taken over. When you British are ruined you stay put, these days, and the National Health looks after your other troubles. The last Church of England vicar of Pau retired seven years ago, and it's difficult to get a really nice cup of tea.

That was the wide-angle view. Looking at it from the middle distance, our village is in the region called Languedoc. Beyond the right-hand frontier of Languedoc, on the far side of the Rhône, is Provence. Inland, Provence is just like Languedoc, except that its towns are a little more picturesque, and it has a much better press, thanks to an army of writers and artists. Aix-en-Provence is where Cézanne did most of his painting, Van Gogh cut off his ear at Arles, and Marcel Pagnol made a lot of films there that keep going the rounds of film societies with Raimu and Fernandel and other actors who are thought of as being very Provençal. Languedocians have never been in fashion like that, and we're jealous. Britons who settle in Provence have more money. They tend to put in swimming pools and full central heating. They need the heating, because when the prevailing – very prevailing – north wind, the mistral, whistles down through Provence in winter, the thermometer may say it's as warm as London, but it doesn't feel like it. Our village is a long way from the mistral, on the right, and a long way from the tramontane, too, on the left, near the Spanish border. We do have a modest north wind, and prevailing is certainly the right word for it, but it doesn't rise to much above sixty miles per hour as it blows the clouds away across the Mediterranean, and so you can spare a hand to clutch your hat. In Provence if you don't grab something more earthbound with both hands you take off.

Over on the left there's the Mediterranean end of the Pyrenees, and beyond them you get to Spain. There are quite a lot of Britons over the frontier, including escaped convicts, and many of them clump together in purpose-built villages called *urbanizacions*, where you get sea and sun and that sort of thing, and where you can live for ten years without speaking a word of the native language – rather like memsahibs in India in the days of the Empire.

The Britons you come across in Languedoc are a different kettle of fish. Perhaps because we can't rise to conspicuous consumption, we like to think we merge into the background. We're snooty about people putting in swimming pools, and the last thing we want is a lot of other Britons moving into our little habitat. We tell tall stories to potential house-buyers about scorpions and wild boars, both of which do exist and can be seen – with luck, once in a blue moon – and Languedocian tarantulas, which are a figment of the imagination. We tell people they'd be much better off in Provence or the Dordogne or Bournemouth. Still, it's hard to find a village that hasn't got a house or a hovel, kept together by do-it-yourself activities, occupied for at least part of the year by *des Anglais*. And we get fiercely chauvinistic about the villages we live in. Ours, for example, really is much better than more picturesque ones elsewhere because it's a real working village, and will go on being so as long as the rest of France and the world go on drinking the wine my neighbours make. Up in the hills you find villages where the only natives are the grandparents of people who have left to earn a decent living in big towns; in winter, when Parisians and other foreigners have mostly gone home after their holidays, life – such as it is – goes on in secret round the TV set.

Coming to a close-up view, I will reveal that our county – or rather *département*, because they tried to do away with counts in the Revolution – is called the Hérault, that being the name of the river that flows through it. We're right in the middle.

At the northern edge of the *département* you get dramatic mountains, the strongholds of Protestants in the days when they were persecuted, and of resistance bands during the last war – all rather deserted these days except in summer, as I've said. But in the foothills there's a funny little spa called Lamalou-les-Bains. French spas keep going because of the French National Health Service. With luck, it will subsidise a spell of convalescence at a nice spa if you can persuade your doctor to recommend it. That makes an agreeable cheap extra holiday. Most spas are full of elderly people with rheumatism or livers, which makes for an absence of the swinging life. Lamalou is different. Its speciality is restoring accident victims to flexible activity by making them do exercises in the therapeutic waters that gush up in the baths. So you see large numbers of young people who've fallen over on their skis or bumped into something in their Porsches, scuttling along on aluminium crutches from pastry shop to café or restaurant and looking remarkably cheerful. A plaster cast is no bar to romance. There's a bandstand on summer evenings, and a festival of fine old fuddy-duddy operettas like *The Merry Widow*, *The Land of Smiles* and *The Student Prince*.

That's north of us. Drive twenty miles south of us, and you reach a great lagoon, ten miles long and a mile wide, where they cultivate oysters – thousands of tons a year. They cement little ones to wooden stakes, which are suspended by wires from long beams. Then they pop round the lagoon in little motor-boats, hauling up the wires to see how the oysters are doing, and perhaps having a swim if the water's nice and warm. And then in the fullness of time they harvest them. Delicious, and about a pound a dozen at the fish shop. The French eat vast quantities of oysters, from here or from the Atlantic coast, and one of the pleasures of going native is that you can have a refreshing mid-morning snack of half a dozen with a glass of local white wine, and feel, like Sam Weller, that oysters and poverty go well together. Why the British oyster has moved up into the caviar class I've no idea. There's a fascinating research station down there, where they breed baby oysters, raise tropical fish and do praise-worthy experiments with sewage and plankton. The public relations person at this institute is an Englishman, partly because they get scientific visitors from all over the world, and these days everyone from Japan to Tel Aviv speaks English, except the French, who are as lazy at languages as the British. He came down here first when he was sixteen, on a school exchange, fell in love with the place, and ten years later landed himself this job, found a wife and became a pillar of the local rugby team.

Drive east from the village and in an hour you're in Montpellier. Before the war it was a quiet little university town – Rabelais studied medicine there – but has shot up in the last twenty years to become what they call a technopolis, with an international airport and a traffic problem. Well, it would have one, wouldn't it? – with all those people who left their mountain villages, came here, prospered and bought cars for all the family.

Going from our village in the opposite direction you come to a little town called Pézenas. Our Arthur Young spent a night here in 1787 and reported in his book *Travels in France* that it was a fine town but that he was put off his dinner at the hotel by the fact that his waitress had such dirty feet. The hotel is still in business and I often have quite a good lunch there. I'm glad to say that the waitress now wears shoes.

If you go window-shopping at half a dozen pastry shops in Pézenas you see, among the éclairs, mille-feuilles and babas au rhum, some strange objects looking like miniature pork pies, about two inches high and an inch across. These are the *petits pâtés de Pézenas*. They're an acquired taste, which is another way of saying they're rather nasty but you can get used to them if you serve them in the right way, which is slightly warm at the beginning of a meal. The filling is made of minced mutton, suet, brown sugar, raisins and lemon peel. Yes, you've got it: they're the ancestor of our present British mince pie. Mrs Beeton, in a 100-year-old edition, gives a similar recipe, but says that many people prefer more modern recipes that leave out the meat, transforming the mince pie into something for the pudding course. I've found out how these little pies got there. Twenty-one years before Arthur Young, in 1766 to be exact, Milord Clive of India rented a château just outside the town, for a self-catering holiday. Those were civilised days; he needed some rest and recuperation after defeating the French in India, and professional activities such as that didn't stop French gentlemen being polite to English gentlemen and vice versa. Anyway, he brought his valet and footmen with him, of course, and his Indian cook who had learnt to make proper meaty mince pies. Clive invited the local gentry to nice little suppers in his holiday château. The conversation must have gone like this:
– Very *intéressants*, Milord, zees leetle *pâtés*. Vat are zey?
– Mince pies. Very traditional. We eat a lot of them at Christmas. Cromwell and the Puritans tried to stamp them out, but they came back with Charles II. Have another.

– Zankyouverimoch. Could I please have ze recipe?

– Well, that's not the kind of thing I know myself. But if you send your cook round to see my cook . . .

So this medieval speciality, forgotten on its home ground, has tunnelled under the Channel and re-surfaced in the Boulevard Jean-Jaurès down in the Midi to give a strange pleasure to archaeological gastronomists.

Pézenas has another speciality. It's the game of tambourin. It's five-a-side tennis, played on a big car-park with a line painted across the middle instead of a net. It uses a hard rubber ball, and instead of a racquet you have a sort of big tambourine without bells. It makes a most satisfying loud clonk as they send the ball high in the air, as high as a two-storey house. The server's tambourine is mounted on a long handle, which he exchanges for an ordinary one after the launch. It's played only in a fifteen-mile radius of Pézenas, and in parts of Tuscany. Every year there's an international, either in Pézenas or in Tuscany, and the Italians usually win because the tambourine-playing area is larger there with more teams clonking away.

As you see, we simple Languedoc folk have simple pleasures. For champagne cocktails and truffles with everything, you'd be better off in Saint-Tropez or in one of those Provençal villages where the clients at the tastefully rustic bistros wear stone-washed designer jeans and speak at maximum volume in the accents of Paris or of the Surrey stockbroker belt.

GRUMBLES

*S*urely,' a listener wrote to me the other day, 'surely there must be a few flies in the ointment? There you are, lazing in the shade with a cooling drink, trying to make us all jealous – but aren't you ever jealous of *us*?'

Good heavens yes. And first of all, if I *am* sitting in the shade with a cooling drink, it's because it's too darn hot to do anything else. My wife Sophie tells me I ought to be writing something, in the hope of earning a little money to pay for those cooling drinks. But when I try the paper keeps sticking to my arms and sweat drips into the typewriter, causing rust because of the high salt content. I've never been much further north in my life than Hampstead NW3, but I know where all the Best People are at this time of year: up in the Highlands of Scotland, picnicking in the heather. That's where that sensible woman Queen Victoria would have been. She used to come down to the Midi in February whenever she could, but in August she was up at Balmoral where cabers can be tossed in cool comfort.

In fact there's a lot to be said for the nice temperate British climate which is so good for the complexion. It's true that we get twice as much sunshine as you do, and that rope-soled sandals are more useful than wellies, but basically we have two types of weather: too hot and too cold. From February to June it keeps flipping from winter to summer and back again, and it does the same from October to December. Instead of a nice gentle drizzle, twice a week all the year round, our annual rainfall – which is the same as London's – comes in three or four giant bucketfuls a year, with thunder, lightning and sometimes hail. Hail is always reported in the local paper as being as big as pigeons' eggs. I've never seen a pigeon's egg, and I bet none of the paper's journalists have either. Our hailstones are in fact about the size of big juicy sweet British peas. And there's another grumble. The French only go in for tiny tasteless peas, the smaller the dearer, and they're only worth eating if you jolly them up with chopped onions and bits of bacon.

That has brought us on to the subject of food, which is well known to be a French invention, like sexual intercourse, the guillotine, and Value Added Tax. The segment of the British population that claims to love France and can afford to go there fairly often tends to be slightly or seriously overweight, and their kitchen shelves groan under the works of Elizabeth David and Jane Grigson. The only book published in France stocked by the average British bookshop is the Michelin guide to French restaurants and hotels. Well, yes, it's true that many of the older generation in France, like our Dr Johnson, take their bellies very seriously, and that top chefs like Bocuse of Lyons, Daguin of Auch and Maximin of Nice get the same kind of treatment in the press and on TV as opera singers and centre-forwards. Such cooks are indeed reliable, though you have to book a month in advance and pay almost London expense-account prices to eat under their auspices. And there are still a few family-run restaurants in country districts where Father does the cooking, Auntie does the washing-up, Uncle grows the vegetables and Grandma feeds the chickens, and if I go on much longer I shall be in danger of giving away my *bonnes petites adresses*. But let's have no illusions about French home cooking today. It's true that there are places like the village I live in, backward old-fashioned places, where old ladies spend four hours a day at the stove doing the kind of thing Elizabeth David wrote about. But nowadays the average French person lives in a big town, and believe it or not the average time she or he takes on food preparation is less than half an hour a day.

Almost all French toddlers go to State nursery schools from the age of two, and then their mother can start earning money again. When she's bought a video-recorder, a microwave is next on the list. Three-quarters of food eaten at home comes ready-prepared from a factory. The deep-freeze section in hypermarkets is a wonderful sight, with all those expertly designed labels, many of them bearing the signature of a famous chef who has given a few suggestions to the food engineers at the mighty factory. The stuff isn't bad, actually, and the average French family keeps going quite healthily on it, but conventional British illusions about what goes on in normal French kitchens are no nearer reality than the conventional French belief that London is perpetually shrouded in a dense yellow fog in which the inhabitants know they are near a school because of the monotonous swish of the cat o' nine tails.

And do the French young yearn for *boeuf bourguignon*, *coq au vin* and *tripes à la mode de Caen*? Not a bit of it. What they want are hamburgers, chips, Coca-Cola, and no waiting. You can't get that sort of thing in our village. Young Jacques Estelle – he's ten – went to England last year on a school visit, and he loved it. 'The sun shone!' he said. 'It was quite warm in London! And we walked across Hyde Park *on the grass*! And there were people flying kites, and we saw a squirrel!' But what about the dreaded British food? He loved that too. From my point of view, the French are still near the top in the dinner league, but from Jacques' point of view – and the Estelles are an old-fashioned family – it's two long boring meals a day, and you have to behave properly, and there's nothing in between. But in England, he found, those two meals were over in a flash like a French breakfast. He simply adored baked beans on toast.

And then there were elevenses and tea. Of course, British factory-made cakes aren't as nice as real éclairs and fresh fruit tarts from the *pâtisserie* in our market town, but he only gets those as the pudding course at Sunday lunch, whereas in England you get cakes every day. And every British child is entitled to a daily quarter of a pound of sweets, with bags of crisps in between . . . Experiences like that improve my image with the village young, so that they ring confidently at our door when they want a hand with their English homework. It's true that Jacques was a little disappointed by the English breakfast. I'd been lending him tourist leaflets before he left, with coloured photographs that suggest you all sit down in your thatched cottages to cornflakes AND grapefruit AND kippers AND bacon and eggs AND sausages every morning. But did you know that a recent survey showed that twenty-seven per cent of Parisians eat nothing at all for breakfast? And that one per cent actually drink their breakfast in the bath? – presumably served by one of the thirty-two point six per cent who have theirs standing up in the kitchen.

One of the sad things about living in France is that there is a total shortage of crumpets. They haven't even got a word for them. I haven't had one for years, and to me they're one of the glories of *la cuisine britannique*, very acceptable for breakfast too, with a couple of rashers on top and melted bacon fat instead of butter. Come to that, there are no toasting forks, and no cheerful buttery tête-à-têtes round the gas fire. No buttered toast even. It's true that you can sometimes find a sort of wrapped sliced bread in the exotic foods section of monster hypermarkets, but the normal long crusty French loaf that the bakers sell warm from the oven twice a day, and which is an essential part of French life, is absolutely useless if you want a nice comforting pile of buttered toast. The holes are too big, for one thing. And it produces a most outlandish sandwich. They call it *un sandwich*, but it's a nine-inch-long cylinder, some three inches in diameter, split lengthways to get the filling in. No human jaw can open wide enough to bite through it in one go. You can try thumping it to flatten it, but usually you end up by taking it apart on a plate and breaking off convenient morsels, and you need both hands and a wash afterwards.

Lord Sandwich was a keen gambler, and he invented the thing so that he could eat it unstickily with one hand without taking his eyes off his cards. It's really shocking, how the French have taken his name in vain.

Enough about food. What about the intellectual life? A great deal of that goes on in France, with half a dozen big politico-literary weekly papers, literary prizes that cause such a well-publicised agitation and brouhaha that our Booker Prize seems a quiet private tea party in comparison, and a lot of books are written, published and bought. Bought, not borrowed, at least not from public libraries, and there's another fly in the ointment. I hope you realise how lucky you are. I've lived most of my life near one-horse market towns. In Cornwall the little library was open thirty-five hours a week, and they would get books for you through the central system. In a comparable town near here they open for a couple of hours four times a week and there's no central system. They seem to get their books from the bargain remainder shop. In the UK one knows that the complete works of Dickens or Scott or George Eliot or Dostoevsky or Balzac are bound to be in the library, and one day one will read them. Perhaps. Anyway, there's no need to buy them, just in case the impulse might seize one some time next year. I'm looking forward to reading all the way through Balzac one day. A reasonable bout of 'flu is enough for three or four volumes, or with a protracted terminal illness I might be able to deal with the lot. Well, they've got just three minor novels by Balzac in our library. On the other hand there are no fewer than fifty paperback Barbara Cartlands, in translation. She does a splendid job for the British balance of payments situation, but I think she would agree that she isn't Balzac. If one day you want to read all through the great French classics, in French, stay in the UK and get them through your local library.

Then there's the television, about which the French themselves are vigorous grumblers. I won't repeat what they say, especially as I rather like French TV because I enjoy seeing old films. They show a lot of those. But there are peculiarities. One is that there are two State channels, paid for by licence fees, but there are as many advertisements on them as on the private channels. The other is that they can't keep on time. What happens is this. The paper says that there's a fine old film at say a quarter to ten. You switch on at a quarter to ten, and there's something else. All right, you think, perhaps there was a panel game earlier which over-ran, or a chat show where the chairman couldn't stop the flow. At ten the advertisements start, three about perfume, four about cheese and two about shampoo. At ten past ten, hallo, there's a trailer for the fine old film you want to see. And the trailer says that it is going to be shown at a quarter to ten on Wednesday. Have we got it wrong, then? It can't be Wednesday today. Or it can't be ten past ten now . . . But domestic research shows that it *is* Wednesday, and the clock isn't wrong . . . After the trailer there are the results of two different kinds of State lottery, three more advertisements for cheese, and for a change one each for a motor-car, a sparkling non-alcoholic drink and a brand of cat food. At last, there's the film. And we had thought we would be in bed before midnight. Tomorrow we shall hear the gnashing of Henri Poujol's teeth. He's just bought a video-recorder and he told us he was going to set it to record the film automatically because he had to go out. Now he's got forty minutes of cheese and so forth, and an appetising trailer for the film he's lost the last third of.

Now what else can I grumble about in this country village? There's noise, of course. In the spring the nightingales turn up, busily performing twenty-four hours a day to mark out their nesting territory. There are a lot of them, because they spend the shooting season safely on the other side of the Mediterranean practising new tunes far from a village shot-gun. The season of *la chasse* is the time when the hills are alive with the sound of locals firing away at everything tasty from thrushes to wild boar. The nightingales come back when it's over, and whistle rudely at the chasseurs. These gentlemen (almost all the able-bodied males of the village) pretend to take no notice. They still go roving in the hills of the garrigue at nightingale time because they know where to find wild asparagus, whose tips make nice omelettes. I'm just teasing you, really. Thanks to Keats and that wartime song about Berkeley Square, we British are nuts about nightingales. They're welcome . . .

Cicadas come later, and they're a different proposition of Nature. The first time we heard them it was alarming. We were coming down a mountain in the Massif Central, towards the Midi, in July, and we thought something had gone wrong in the engine: big ends falling apart or piston rings tangling with the tappets. We stopped, and switched off. The racket went on. It was them. You can't see cicadas until you get used to looking for them: they are green when they come out of their holes, and a couple of inches long, but they soon turn brown and blend in with the trees on which they sit. And they stridulate madly all day long unless there's a cloud in front of the sun, which isn't often. That fable by La Fontaine is called 'The Grasshopper and the Ant' in English, but La Fontaine was writing about *cigales*, or cicadas, and noise-wise what a flute is to a trombone, a grasshopper is to a cicada. In the avenue of plane trees that leads to the village the noise is deafening. They spend four long years burrowing tunnels underground, nibbling at roots to keep themselves going. Then one night in June they come out from their holes, shed their outer skins, unfold their new bodies, climb up the olive trees and the pines and the plane trees, and start squeaking and copulating. They're quite defenceless: birds and lizards eat them, but strangely enough the French have not yet found a recipe for them. *Saga, saga, saga* is what the locals say they're chirruping in patois, and that means 'Get reaping the wheat' because the corn is ripe when they emerge. Four years down the mine, one summer holiday of sun, sex and song, and that's their lot. Would you rather be an ant? When night falls the cicadas shut up, and the frogs start in the reservoir by the allotments. Never a quiet moment.

A much more traumatic noise started last year. It's a monotonous thump, thump, thump-thump-thump, above which the sound of an uncouth person apparently shouting insults can sometimes be heard. It starts at about nine in the evening, and it can go on until two or three in the morning on special occasions. This is *les jeunes*, listening to music on their 100-watt amplifier. Before I go on, I must explain about *les jeunes*.

To make a wild generalisation, smallish children are nicer in France than their contemporaries in Britain. The ones in our little primary school, which I told you about earlier, are especially civilised because of their teacher, Madame Martin, who has only ten pupils to take care of, and whose views on child psychology and a pleasant life are entirely in harmony with those of the village parents. Most French children of that age are harmless, friendly and even a pleasure to have around the place. They are known as *les petits*, or *les petitouns* in our patois. They say *Monsieur* or *Madame*, and *Merci* and *S'il vous plaît*, and shake hands properly. They stay up later than British children as long as they aren't a nuisance to their elders and betters. British parents pander to small children and then pack them off to bed with a sigh of relief; grown-up pleasures, such as conversation, can then start. *Les petits* are trained not to interfere with civilised activities.

And then time passes, and *les petits* turn into *les jeunes*, and on the whole they come lower on the scale of civilisation than their British opposite numbers. The French expect this. They say, with a gesture of helplessness, '*Il faut que jeunesse passe*', as though youth were something like mumps or measles: a bother, but natural and to be put up with. A young French person remains a *jeune* until he or she becomes *sérieux*, which doesn't mean serious but responsible. Some people become *sérieux* as early as sixteen. With others it's a longer process. Anyway, it's accepted that a *jeune* has to *faire des bêtises* – do stupid things. The older a *jeune* is, the more people hope he or she will *faire ses bêtises* somewhere else, in another village or another quarter of the town, but with younger *jeunes* there's a certain amount of anxiety if they take to zooming off on their mopeds with the air of being about to *faire une bêtise*. Anyway, parents check their third-party insurance. You don't *have* to have third-party insurance if you're a parent, but as French law makes you responsible for any damage your offspring cause to other people or their property, having children who are under the age of majority is dangerous. It's like having a car or a shot-gun or a tiger, and you take out a policy and hope that a *bêtise* won't lose you your no-claims bonus.

Anyhow, our *jeunes* – there are four of them – were complaining bitterly last year that there was nothing for them in the village, not even a café with a pin-ball machine, and they always had to go off somewhere else for a bit of what they call life. So the municipal council gave them the use of quite a decent shed, a hundred yards from our house, and a machine for reproducing cassettes and discs at enormous volume. There's a law in France against *tapage nocturne*, which is making a noise that other people can hear after half-past ten at night, but the council seems to be afraid of *les jeunes*, or at least doesn't want them to zoom off on mopeds to an unknown fate. The law against *tapage nocturne* admits of frequent exceptions, such as fêtes, and nobody wants to be a spoil-sport. However, other *jeunes* have recently taken to turning up from other villages, intent on making their *bêtises* here. I wonder what will happen. In France things usually go on until something awful occurs, and then there's a dramatic crack-down. Some of the so-called songs appear to be in a sort of degenerate English – though as the singers can't enunciate properly, I'm not sure.

I was looking the other day in Lemprière's *Classical Dictionary*, 1832 edition. There the Satyrs are described as 'A hairy race of monsters, who made dancing and playing on musical instruments their chief study'. Under the entry 'Satyrs' I learnt that 'one was brought to Sylla, as that general returned from Thessaly. The monster had been surprised asleep in a cave; but its voice was inarticulate, and Sylla was so disgusted with it that he ordered it to be instantly removed.' Good for him. I know how he felt. And in his time they didn't have 100-watt amplifiers, with bass-boosters to communicate the beat through the foundations. There are signs that other villagers' nerves will crack before mine do, and then something will be done about the volume control, and we shall be able to hear the frogs again. This kind of noise is described in intellectual French newspapers as an example of what they call 'Anglo-Saxon Cultural Imperialism'. Golly.

Ah well, one of the pleasures of life is having a good grumble. These days, when most things from fishfingers to pop music are much the same from Buenos Aires to Helsinki, it's nice to zip from time to time from France to England and vice versa. There are still a few different things to grumble about. Look forward to your crumpet season! I'll go and see if the nightingales are still at it.